RESTORING AND RENEWING THE PEOPLE OF GOD

A Study of Ezra & Nehemiah

Jack W. Hayford
with
Joseph Snider

THOMAS NELSON PUBLISHERS
Nashville

Restoring and Renewing the People of God
A Study of Ezra & Nehemiah
Copyright © 1998 by Jack W. Hayford

Published in Nashville, Tennessee, by Thomas Nelson, Inc.

Unless otherwise indicated, Scripture quotations are from the
New King James Version of the Bible, © 1979, 1980, 1982,
Thomas Nelson, Inc., Publishers

Printed in the United States of America
1 2 3 4 5 6 7 8 — 03 02 01 00 99 98

CONTENTS

Restoring and Renewing the People of God (A Study of Ezra & Nehemiah) is one of a series of study guides that focus exciting, discovery-geared coverage of Bible book and power themes—all prompting toward dynamic, Holy Spirit-filled living.

About the Executive Editor

JACK W. HAYFORD, noted pastor, teacher, writer, and composer, is the Executive Editor of the complete series, working with the publisher in conceiving and developing each of the books.

Dr. Hayford is Senior Pastor of The Church On The Way, the First Foursquare Church of Van Nuys, California. He and his wife, Anna, have four married children, all of whom are active in either pastoral ministry or vital church life. As General Editor of the *Spirit-Filled Life® Bible*, Pastor Hayford led a four-year project which has resulted in the availability of one of today's most practical and popular study Bibles. He is author of more than twenty books, including *A Passion for Fullness, The Beauty of Spiritual Language, Rebuilding the Real You*, and *Prayer Is Invading the Impossible*. His musical compositions number over four hundred songs, including the widely sung "Majesty."

About the Writer

JOSEPH SNIDER is director of family ministries for Fellowship Missionary Church in Fort Wayne, Indiana. His knowledge of the Bible has been sharpened through experience as a youth evangelist with Young Life in Dallas, a faculty member of Fort Wayne Bible College (now Taylor University, Fort Wayne), and three pastoral positions in Indiana in addition to several years of freelance writing.

Married to Sally Snider, Joe has two grown children, Jenny and Ted. They live in Indianapolis, Indiana. Joe earned a B.A. in English from Cedarville College in Cedarville, Ohio, and a Th.M. in Christian Education from Dallas Theological Seminary.

Of this contributor, the General Editor has remarked: "Joe Snider's strength and stability as a gracious, godly man comes through in his writing. His perceptive and practical way of pointing the way to truth inspires students of God's Word."

THE GIFT
THAT KEEPS ON GIVING

One of the most precious gifts God has given us is His Word, the Bible. Wrapped in the glory and sacrifice of His Son and delivered by the power and ministry of His Spirit, it is a treasured gift—the gift that keeps on giving, because the Giver it reveals is inexhaustible in His love and grace.

Tragically, though, fewer and fewer people are opening this gift and seeking to understand what it's all about and how to use it. They often feel intimidated by it. It requires some assembly, and its instructions are hard to comprehend sometimes. How does the Bible fit together anyway? What does this ancient Book have to say to us who are looking toward the twenty-first century? Will taking the time and energy to understand its instructions and to fit it all together really help you and me?

Yes. Yes. Without a shred of doubt.

The *Spirit-Filled Life® Bible Discovery Guide* series is designed to help you unwrap, assemble, and enjoy all God has for you in the pages of Scripture. It will focus your time and energy on the books of the Bible, the people and places they describe, and the themes and life applications that flow thick from its pages like honey oozing from a beehive.

So you can get the most out of God's Word, this series has a number of helpful features:

 WORD WEALTH

"WORD WEALTH" provides definitions of key terms.

BEHIND THE SCENES

"BEHIND THE SCENES" supplies information about cultural practices, doctrinal disputes, business trades, etc.

AT A GLANCE

"AT A GLANCE" features helpful maps and charts.

BIBLE EXTRA

"BIBLE EXTRA" will guide you to other resources that will enable you to glean more from the Bible's wealth.

PROBING THE DEPTHS

"PROBING THE DEPTHS" will explain controversial issues raised by particular lessons and cite Bible passages and other sources to help you come to your own conclusions.

FAITH ALIVE

The "FAITH ALIVE" feature will help you see and apply the Bible to your day-to-day needs.

As you'll see, these guides supply space for you to answer the study and life-application questions and exercises. You may, however, want to record all your answers, or just the overflow from your study or application, in a separate notebook or journal. This would be especially helpful if you think you'll dig into the BIBLE EXTRA features. Because the exercises in this feature are optional and can be expanded as far as you want to take them, we have not allowed writing space for them in this study guide. So you may want to have a notebook or journal handy for recording your discoveries while working through this feature's riches.

The Bible study method used in this series revolves around four basic steps: observation, interpretation, correlation, and application. Observation answers the question, What does the text say? Interpretation deals with, What does the text mean?—not with what it means to you or me, but what it meant to its original readers. Correlation asks, What light do other Scripture passages shed on this text? And application, the goal of Bible study, poses the question, How should my life change in response to the Holy Spirit's teaching of this text?

If you have used a Bible much before, you know that it comes in a variety of translations and paraphrases. Although you can use any of them with profit as you work through the *Spirit-Filled Life® Bible Discovery Guide* series, when Bible passages or words are cited, you will find they are from the New King James Version of the Bible. Using this translation with this series will make your study easier, but it's certainly not necessary.

The only resources you need to complete and apply these study guides are a heart and mind open to the Holy Spirit, a prayerful attitude, and a pencil and a Bible. Of course, you may draw upon other sources, but these study guides are comprehensive enough to give you all you need to gain a good, basic understanding of the Bible book being covered and how you can apply its themes and counsel to your life.

A word of warning, though. By itself, Bible study will not transform your life. It will not give you power, peace, joy, comfort, hope, and a number of other gifts God longs for you to unwrap and enjoy. Through Bible study, you will grow in your understanding of the Lord, His kingdom and your place in it, but you must be sure to rely on the Holy Spirit to guide your study and your application of the Bible's truths. He, Jesus promised, was sent to teach us "all things" (John 14:26; cf. 1 Cor. 2:13). Bathe your study time in prayer, asking the Spirit of God to illuminate the text, enlighten your mind, humble your will, and comfort your heart. He will never let you down.

My prayer and goal for you is that as you unwrap and begin to explore God's Book for living His way, the Holy Spirit will fill every fiber of your being with the joy and power God longs to give all His children. So read on. Be diligent. Stay open and submissive to Him. You will not be disappointed. He promises you!

Restoring and Renewing Worship
(Ezra 1—6)

God chastened His people Israel seventy years in Babylon because they had repeatedly and persistently rejected His rule over their lives. When that period of chastening ended and the Lord set out to reestablish His covenant people in the land He had promised them, He did not begin by restoring and renewing their political establishment. His first priority was not restoring and renewing their economy. It was not restoring and renewing education, housing, or transportation.

The sovereign God restored and renewed the worship of His people as the first stage of reestablishing them as a nation. Whenever our lives feel ineffective or stale, whenever we have experienced the chastening of the Lord, whenever we want to reach a greater level of intimacy with our Lord, the first priority must be rebuilding or strengthening our worship of the living God. The Holy Spirit makes His dwelling and His base of operation in hearts given to worship.

Lesson 1/A Second Exodus
Ezra 1—2

William Bradford was the first governor of the Plymouth Bay Colony founded in 1620 by the Pilgrims who landed on Cape Cod in the *Mayflower*. Bradford's personal history of the first several years of the colony disappeared from Boston's Old North Church during the American Revolution and "turned up" in 1855 in the library of the Bishop of London. England returned the manuscript to Massachussetts in 1897.

In his ninth chapter, Governor Bradford imagined the children of the original Pilgrims making this confession: "Our faithers were Englishmen which came over this great ocean, and were ready to perish in this willdernes; but they cried unto the Lord, and he heard their voyce, and looked on their adversitie, etc. Let them therfore praise the Lord, because he is good, and his mercies endure for ever. Yea, let them which have been redeemed of the Lord, shew how he has delivered them from the hand of the oppressour. When they wandered in the deserte willdernes out of the way, and found no citie to dwell in, both hungrie, and thirstie, their sowle was overwhelmed in them. Let them confess before the Lord his loving kindness, and his wonderfull works before the sons of men" (*Of Plimouth Plantation*).[1]

William Bradford likened the settling of Plymouth by the Pilgrims to the Exodus of Israel from Egypt. But before the governor ever thought of the Pilgrim flight from persecution in England as a second Exodus, the Bible itself pointed to another second Exodus—Israel's deliverance from the Babylonian captivity (see, for example, Is. 43:14–21). Once again Israel had been enslaved in a foreign land—Babylon. Once again God moved a foreign potentate—Cyrus the Persian—to release His people. Once more they skirted a desert to reach the Promised Land.

WHO, WHAT, WHEN, AND WHERE IN ANCIENT PERSIA

The era of the Persian Empire is well known from extra-biblical writings and from extensive archaeological evidence. Persia replaced Babylon as the major power in the ancient Near East after the Medo-Persian armies under Cyrus's control conquered Babylon. The southern kingdom of Judah had been captured and deported by the Babylonians. The Jewish exiles dispersed through portions of the Babylonian Empire became the responsibility of the Persian conquerors.

Jeremiah had predicted that the Babylonian captivity of Judah would last seventy years (Jer. 25:12; 29:10) while the land of Palestine rested (2 Chr. 36:21). Look up the following passages and identify the events that could mark the beginning or end of the seventy years.

- 605 B.C. (2 Kin. 23:36—24:4; Dan. 1:1–6)

- 597 B.C. (2 Kin. 24:8–16; Jer. 29:1–10)

- 586 B.C. (1 Kin. 25:1–12; Jer. 39:1, 2)

- 538 B.C. (2 Chr. 36:22, 23; Ezra 1:1–4)

- 515 B.C. (Ezra 6:14–18)

Jeremiah first predicted the seventy-year captivity in 605 B.C. (Jer. 25:10, 11) and Daniel, who was deported at that time, was given insight into the meaning of the number (Dan. 9:1, 2). Perhaps the seventy years stretched from that minor deportation in 605 B.C. to Cyrus's decree authorizing the return in 538 B.C., a span of sixty-eight years. Or the seventy years might have begun with the destruction of the temple in 586 B.C. and ended with its reconstruction in 515 B.C., a period of seventy-one years. The second option seems tidier, but Cyrus's decree in 538 B.C. seems to mark the end of the captivity (Is. 44:28; Ezra 1:1). Most Bible students conclude that seventy was a round number indicating a full lifetime of punishment. Identifying a specific seventy-year span with certainty is difficult.

Look up the following passages and identify the four Persian emperors who figure in biblical history.

1. _____ 538–530 B.C. (Ezra 1:1)

2. _____ 521–486 B.C. (Ezra 4:5; 5:5—6:15)

3. _____ 486–465 B.C. (Ezra 4:6; Esth. 1—10)

4. _____ 464–424 B.C. (Ezra 4:7–23; 7:1–26; Neh. 2:1; 13:6)

The Persian Empire stretched from the Indus River in India to the upper reaches of the Nile in Africa and northern Greece in Europe. Darius divided the empire into 23 divisions known as satrapies. The satrapies subdivided into 127 provinces (Esth. 1:1). Persia boasted four capital cities: Babylon, Susa (called Shushan in Neh. 1:1), Ecbatana (called Achmetha in Ezra 6:2), and Persepolis (not mentioned in the Bible). Judah was part of the fifth satrap, "Beyond the River" (the Euphrates).

 AT A GLANCE

Note that the Persian and Greek empires extended to the broken line border, from Libya in the west to India in the east and Thrace in the north.

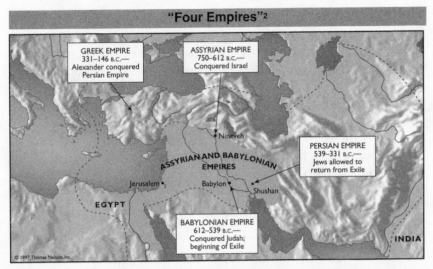

"Four Empires"[2]

GREEK EMPIRE
331–146 B.C.—
Alexander conquered
Persian Empire

ASSYRIAN EMPIRE
750–612 B.C.—
Conquered Israel

PERSIAN EMPIRE
539–331 B.C.—
Jews allowed to
return from Exile

ASSYRIAN AND BABYLONIAN EMPIRES

Nineveh

Jerusalem •

Babylon •

Shushan •

EGYPT

BABYLONIAN EMPIRE
612–539 B.C.—
Conquered Judah;
beginning of Exile

INDIA

© 1997 Thomas Nelson, Inc.

The events of Ezra and Nehemiah spanned more than a century. Look up the following passages and record the key event mentioned in each.

- (538 B.C.) (Ezra 2:1)

- (537 B.C.) (Ezra 3:3)

- (536 B.C.) (Ezra 3:10–12)

- (515 B.C.) (Ezra 6:15)

- (458 B.C.) (Ezra 7:8, 9)

- (445 B.C.) (Neh. 1:1–4)

- (445 B.C.) (Neh. 6:15)

- (445 B.C.) (Neh. 12:27, 43)

FAITH ALIVE

Ezra and Nehemiah tell the story of a new beginning for the people of God after a time of judgment for sin. Through this time God raised up leaders to guide, challenge, and inspire His people to follow Him to victory in the face of overwhelming opposition.

Who have been the spiritual leaders God has used to help you recover from times of discouragement or backsliding?

What have you learned about God from the way He has treated you when you have been indifferent to Him?

A TOOL IN GOD'S HAND

Cyrus was one of the great figures of world history. He united the Medes and the Persians. He defeated the mighty Babylonians. He built the greatest world empire that had existed up to his time. If you had interviewed him about his greatest accomplishments, he would not have listed sending the Jews home to Jerusalem among his primary achievements. God did, however.

How do the following indicators reveal that Cyrus's proclamation was very important? (Ezra 1:1)

- Its timing

- Its prophetic preparation

- Its divine initiation

- Its thorough publication

WORD WEALTH

Stirred up translates a Hebrew word meaning to rouse, awaken, stir up, excite, raise up; to incite; to arouse to action; or to open one's eyes. **Stirred up** occurs about seventy-five times in the Old Testament. It applies to an eagle stirring up its nest (Deut. 32:11) and of a musical instrument being warmed up for playing (Ps. 108:2). In Isaiah 50:4 the Lord awakens the prophet each morning and "awakens" his ear to hear God's message. Isaiah 51:9 speaks of the arm of the Lord being roused to action.[3] In the present reference God's Spirit incites the spirit of Cyrus the Persian emperor to carry out the prophesied liberation of His people.

BEHIND THE SCENES

The prophet Isaiah called Cyrus the Lord's shepherd (Is. 44:28) and His anointed (45:1). Cyrus was anointed in the sense that God chose him for a special mission. God, through Isaiah, called Cyrus by name more than one hundred years before his time to prove to the Persian king that He, Yahweh, was the only true God. The Jewish historian Josephus says that Cyrus released Israel when he was shown the prophecy of Isaiah 45.[4]

Summarize the content of Cyrus's decree about these topics.

• Its motivation (Ezra 1:2)

• Its main provision (Ezra 1:3)

• Its advice to spectators (Ezra 1:4)

Cyrus returned many captive peoples to their homelands and rebuilt many of their temples. He thought he was being shrewd. He did not know he was serving the purposes of "the LORD God of heaven" (Ezra 1:2).

Who responded to Cyrus's decree to return to Jerusalem and rebuild the temple of the Lord? (Ezra 1:5)

How did the people surrounding the Jews who were returning to Jerusalem show their support of them? (Ezra 1:6)

Cyrus made it his policy to restore the idols that the Babylonians had looted from various temples around the ancient Near East. The living God forbade His worshipers to make images representing Him (Ex. 20:4, 5). How did Cyrus show his support of the Jews who had no idols? (Ezra 1:7–11)

 BEHIND THE SCENES

Sheshbazzar was called "the prince of Judah" when he received the temple articles from Cyrus in Babylon (Ezra 1:8). Later, he was called the governor of Judah (5:14). Once the Jews arrived in Jerusalem, however, Zerubbabel was the leader they looked to for guidance. In time he became governor in title as well as fact (Hag. 1:1; 2:2). Sheshbazzar may have been an elderly man because he quickly faded from the scene of biblical events.

 FAITH ALIVE

In your opinion, who are the four or five most powerful people in the world? (Don't just limit your thinking to political leaders).

If God chose to, what are some of the things He could do through these people tomorrow?

How do you think the Holy Spirit exerts His influence over powerful people of the world?

PROUD PIONEERS

Most Jews stayed in their comfortable Babylonian homes when Cyrus decreed that all who wanted to could return to Jerusalem at imperial expense and rebuild the temple of the Lord. It took a courageous type who had confidence in God and perhaps a good deal of self-confidence to pull up stakes and head a thousand miles to build a home on a fifty-year-old rubble heap. The names in Ezra 2 are like the passenger manifest of the *Mayflower*. These folks would be remembered forever for daring to do what they did.

What do you imagine each of these facts mentioned in Ezra 2:1 meant to the exiles who first returned to Judah and Jerusalem?

• They were returning to a province of Persia rather than an independent homeland.

• They were leaving captivity.

• They or, more likely, their ancestors had been carried away to Babylon by Nebuchadnezzar.

• They were returning to the cities and villages of their ancestors.

The list of exiles who chose to return to Judah included leaders (Ezra 2:2), laypeople grouped by clans (vv. 3–20), laypeople grouped by hometown (vv. 21–35), priests (vv. 36–39), various groups of Levites (vv. 40–42), temple servants whose names suggest they were of Gentile extraction (vv. 43–58),[5] and those whose genealogy was uncertain (vv. 59–61). Many of the village and city names can be located on the accompanying map.

AT A GLANCE

"POSTEXILIC SAMARIA AND JUDAH"

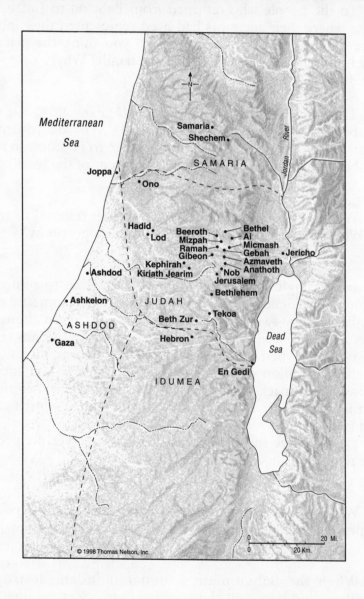

N

Mediterranean
Sea

Samaria
Shechem

SAMARIA

Jordan River

Joppa

Ono

Hadid
Lod

Beeroth
Mizpah
Ramah
Gibeon
Kephirah
Kiriath Jearim

Bethel
Ai
Micmash
Gebah
Azmaveth
Anathoth
Nob

Jericho

Ashdod

Jerusalem
Bethlehem

Ashkelon

JUDAH

Beth Zur
Hebron

Tekoa

Dead
Sea

ASHDOD

Gaza

En Gedi

IDUMEA

0   20 Mi.
0   20 Km.

© 1998 Thomas Nelson, Inc.

What does the list of exiles suggest about the value to God of ordinary people from many different backgrounds in accomplishing His purposes?

To the people who returned from Babylon to Judah, the places where their ancestors had lived represented their inheritance from God. How important do you think the place of your home should be to you and your family? Why?

The returning exiles totaled 42,360 (Ezra 2:64). Of that number 4,289 were priests (vv. 36–39). Why do you think priests would respond to Cyrus's challenge to go home in such numbers that made up more than 10 percent of the total?

What sort of spiritual challenges do you respond to readily? Why are you responsive to that kind of opportunity?

Interestingly, the group of Jews who chose to return to Judah and Jerusalem appears to have contained some wealthy members. Forty-two thousand people owned seven thousand slaves and employed two hundred professional musicians (Ezra 2:65). They owned luxury animals, such as horses, mules, and camels, in addition to large numbers of donkeys, the ancient Volkswagen of pack beasts (vv. 66, 67). From their own number they contributed princely gifts to the temple construction fund (vv. 68, 69).

What unique spiritual truths do you think wealthy people have to grasp to have strong faith in God?

What special responsibilities do you think wealthy people accept who commit themselves wholeheartedly to serve the Lord?

When the Babylonians conquered Judah, destroyed Jerusalem, and deported the population in 586 B.C., they left the poorest peasantry to keep the land from reverting to total wilderness (2 Kin. 25:12). What mix of emotions do you imagine the returning exiles experienced when they arrived in their ancestral communities with their backward populations and depressed economies (Ezra 2:70)?

FAITH ALIVE

What spiritual risk(s) has the Lord led you to take in the past that made you feel like a pioneer for Him? How did the Holy Spirit stir your spirit to want to be a part of this?

What kind of spiritual adventure would you like to be a part of in the future that would make you feel as though you had done something really worthwhile for those who come after you?

1. William Bradford, "Of Plimouth Plantation," *The Literature of the United States* (Chicago: Scott, Foresman and Company, 1957), 32.

2. Adapted from *The Open Bible* (Nashville: Thomas Nelson Publishers, 1997), 1354, map "Four Empires."

3. *Spirit-Filled Life® Bible* (Nashville: Thomas Nelson Publishers, 1991), 1359, "Word Wealth, Hag. 1:14, stirred."

4. Ibid., 1021, note on Is. 45:1–13.

5. Edwin M. Yamauchi, "Ezra-Nehemiah," *The Expositor's Bible Commentary*, Vol. 4 (Grand Rapids: Zondervan Publishing House, 1988), 615.

Lesson 2/Worship Provokes Opposition
Ezra 3—4

It used to be that churches were welcome additions to any neighborhood, rural, urban, or suburban. Times have changed. Urban planners are reluctant to lose more blocks of property from the tax rolls. Suburban neighborhoods object to massive parking lots and the increase in traffic that often accompanies church services.

In some cities laws intended to protect churches are being used to keep them out. It's often illegal to build a bar or exotic dance club within certain distances of a church. Stand those ordinances on their head, and a church cannot be built near bourbon or nude dancers.

Churches often find themselves tangled in expensive, time-consuming litigation before they can buy land or build worship facilities. Once the assumption was that churches were valuable to the moral and spiritual tone of a community. In some places churches seem to be viewed increasingly as consumers of valuable resources that contribute nothing in return.

When the first Jewish exiles returned from Babylon to Jerusalem and Judah, they viewed the worship of the Lord as their first priority. After all, the emperor Cyrus had commissioned them to rebuild the temple and reinstitute the sacrificial system (Ezra 1:3). However, they found that their neighbors in the land were not anxious to see true biblical worship resume. It challenged a social system with which they were comfortable.

WORSHIP STARTS WITH AN ALTAR

Assuming King Cyrus made his decree authorizing the resettlement of Judah and Jerusalem at the very beginning of his first year as ruler of Babylon as well as Persia, the exiles barely had time to arrive by the seventh month (Ezra 3:1). Ezra later would make the journey from Babylon to Jerusalem in four months with a much smaller party (7:9). Jeshua, Zerubbabel, and their multitude of 42,360 settlers (2:64) moved quickly because they had a clear mission. Their priority—as ordered by Cyrus—was worship (1:2–4).

The seventh month of the Jewish calendar contained the Feast of Trumpets (Lev. 23:24), the Day of Atonement (vv. 23–29), and the Feast of Tabernacles (vv. 34–43). What did the exiles do in response to the arrival of the very special seventh month? (Ezra 3:1)

The walls of Jerusalem were still in ruins. The temple area had not been cleaned up or made ready for festivities or ceremonies. What was the very first step the exiles took toward rebuilding their community? (Ezra 3:2)

WORD WEALTH

Altar (Ezra 3:2) translates a Hebrew noun constructed from the verb "to sacrifice." An **altar**, therefore, was a place of sacrifice. The noun occurs more than four hundred times in the Old Testament. **Altars** were very important as the site of the worship of Noah and the patriarchs Abraham, Isaac, and Jacob. In the tabernacle and in Solomon's temple, the bronze **altar** was the center of daily activity, without which the rest of Israel's worship could not take place. The "**altar** of sacrifice" was also crucial in God's revelation of true worship for joyful times, such as feasts.[1]

WORD WEALTH

Law (Ezra 3:2) translates the Hebrew word *torah. Torah* is based on a verb that means "to shoot (an arrow), to cast down in a straight manner, or to direct." The idea is that God's instructions to Israel (the Torah) laid down a straight path to follow to the target of righteous relationships between God and people. This noun occurs 217 times in the Old Testament. Usually the **Law** of God is in view, although the rules and instructions of godly parents are also *torah* (Prov. 1:8; 3:1).[2]

How do you imagine that fear of the surrounding peoples motivated the returned exiles to erect the altar of the Lord? (Ezra 3:3)

Why do you think the exiles were careful to erect their new altar exactly where the one from Solomon's temple had been? (Ezra 3:3; see Deut. 12:13, 14, 27; 2 Sam. 24:18–25; 2 Chr. 6:12; 7:1)

What rituals of worship did the exiles institute immediately on their newly erected altar? (Ezra 3:3, 4, 6)

What rituals of worship did the exiles initiate as the times for them came along? (Ezra 3:5)

KINGDOM EXTRA

Godly living is standing up for what you believe even in the face of hostile opposition. Be faithful to God, and bold in your faith in Him despite the possible hostility of the world around you. Remember that the Lord will honor those who honor Him.[3]

Why do you think the altar was more fundamental to Jewish worship and atonement than the temple? (Ezra 3:6)

WORD WEALTH

Temple (2 Kin. 18:16) translates a Hebrew noun that appears about eighty times in the Old Testament. Basic to this term is the sense of a splendid, regal building fit to be a king's residence. The most natural rendering of this word is "palace," and this reading occurs in passages such as Psalm 45:8 and 15 and Isaiah 39:7. However, in the great majority of occurrences, it refers to the Lord's temple in Jerusalem.[4] This is fitting since the **temple** was the "palace" of "the King, the Lord of hosts" (Is. 6:5) who ruled over His covenant people. Sacrifice at the site of the **temple** revealed the submission of the exiles to their King.

What preliminary arrangements did the leaders of the exilic community make toward the future construction of the temple? (Ezra 3:7)

How did these preparations compare with those of Solomon more than four hundred years earlier? (see 1 Kin. 5:6, 9)

FAITH ALIVE

What are some of the sacrifices the Lord wants us to offer Him on the altars of our hearts? (for example, see Rom. 12:1; Phil. 2:17; 4:18; Heb. 13:15, 16; 1 Pet. 2:5)

When can fear of the threats of the world serve as a positive stimulus for worship? When can that fear become negative and harm your worship?

THE TEMPLE FOUNDATION INSPIRES PRAISE

Once the returned exiles survived their first winter in their makeshift homes in Judah and Jerusalem, they were ready to get down to the business of constructing the temple. So many of their hopes for themselves and their descendants depended on establishing the house of God as the center of their community.

Why would it have been significant to the exiles to start work on the new temple in an official way in the second month? (Ezra 3:8; see 1 Kin. 6:1)

Who had taken the lead in erecting the altar (Ezra 3:2), and who took the lead in starting the temple construction (v. 8)? Why do you suppose each led the way in his respective project?

Who comprised the work force for the temple? Who functioned as the overseeing body? Who were the leaders of the overseers? (Ezra 3:8b, 9)

What was the role of each of these in kicking off the construction of the postexilic temple of the Lord in Jerusalem? (Ezra 3:10)

- The workers

- The Levites

- Long-dead King David

Who did the officials in Persia and the surrounding provinces credit with laying the foundation of the temple? (see Ezra 5:16; compare 1:8)

What do you think the psalm of praise the levitical choirs sang meant to Israel in general and to the returned exiles in particular? (Ezra 3:11; see Ps. 136; Jer. 33:10, 11)

WORD WEALTH

Praising (Ezra 3:11) translates a form of the Hebrew verb *halal*. *Halal* means "to boast about someone," "to thank," "to rejoice." *Halal* usually conveys the idea of speaking or singing about the glories, virtues, or honor of God. This is the root from which "hallelujah" is formed. The phrase *hallelu-Jah* is a command: "All of you must praise the Lord." Also derived from *halal* is *tehillah*, or *tehillim* in the plural. A *tehillah* is a praise, a psalm, or a song. The Hebrew title of the Book of Psalms is *Tehillim*, literally "Praises."[5]

When the official ceremony marking the founding or cornerstone of the temple project ended, how did the onlooking assembly of Israel respond? (Ezra 3:11)

WORD WEALTH

Great shout (Ezra 3:11) translates a Hebrew noun that intensifies the meaning of the normal Hebrew verb "to shout." Consequently the noun means "a shout of joy," "a noisy clamor," "a trumpet blast," or "a victory shout." A **great shout** is an ear-piercing great noise, a sound that cannot be ignored. This was the kind of shout of celebration that welcomed the ark into Jerusalem in David's day.[6]

KINGDOM EXTRA

The exiles shouting with a great shout (Ezra 3:11) is consistent with a kind of worship that is acceptable to the Lord. Periodically, every believer needs to confront in himself or herself anything that would tend toward passivity regarding his or her worship of God. In verses 12 and 13, the volume of the shouting was more than cultural. Something was being established in the spirit as the exiles moved ahead in boldness and were heard "afar off."[7]

In contrast to the multitude who responded to the temple foundation with a great shout, who responded to it with loud weeping? (Ezra 3:12)

BIBLE EXTRA

Look up the following passages from the minor prophets who ministered to the exiles and reconstruct from these later strands of biblical evidence why the older exilic leaders wept when the temple was founded.

- Haggai 2:3

- Zechariah 4:10

Why were loud rejoicing and weeping both understandable responses to the founding of the new temple? (Ezra 3:11, 12)

What kinds of reactions do you suppose distant listeners had to the incredible clamor they heard from the hilltop ruins of Jerusalem? (Ezra 3:13)

FAITH ALIVE

When has the beginning of some work of God moved you to grateful praise? How did you express that praise?

How has Satan hinted to you that some work for the Lord was too small to be important? What did that do to your motivation to serve God?

In recalling how God has shown His mercy and goodness in the past, what events come to your mind from history and from your own experience?

WORLDLINESS STIFLES WORSHIP

The exilic community of Judah was small and powerless in worldly terms, but the people around them did not like the idea of seeing Jerusalem rebuilt and the worship of the Lord reestablished. They soon banded together to explore ways to frustrate the plans of the Jews to carry out the decree of Cyrus and the desires of their heart.

Under what label did the writer of the Book of Ezra introduce the neighbors of the exiles in Judah and Jerusalem? (Ezra 4:1a)

What prompted the neighboring people to send emissaries to Zerubbabel and the elders of Judah and Benjamin? (Ezra 4:1b)

What proposal did the neighbors of Judah, in the old territory of the northern kingdom of Israel, make to the returned exiles? (Ezra 4:2)

What do you think the adversaries of Judah and Benjamin hoped to accomplish by becoming partners in the project to build the temple of the Lord in Jerusalem?

What reason did Zerubbabel and the priest Jeshua give to their northern neighbors for refusing to let them help rebuild the temple? (Ezra 4:3)

BEHIND THE SCENES

In 722 B.C. the northern kingdom of Israel had been conquered by the Assyrian Empire under the command of first Shalmaneser and then Sargon (2 Kin. 17:5, 6). The population was deported to Mesopotamia and replaced with people-groups from various parts of Mesopotamia (v. 24). The resettlement of Israel continued until the time of the Assyrian emperor Esarhaddon (Ezra 4:2).

The worship of the people around Samaria was syncretistic. That means they combined aspects of their native Mesopotamian religions with the idolatrous form of the worship of the Lord that had developed in northern Israel after the time of King Solomon (1 Kin. 17:29–33, 41). The tiny exilic community could never have maintained its identity and focus if it had cooperated with the spiritually corrupt Samarians.

The span of time referred to in Ezra 4:4 and 5 covers sixteen years (536–520 B.C.). What three-step process did the adversaries follow to bring the temple construction to a stop? What do you imagine was involved in each of these steps?

1.

2.

3.

KINGDOM EXTRA

The holy life is separated from the world and set apart to God. Be advised that the world seeks to discourage and frustrate the purposes of God's people. Seek counsel from God and shun the advice of the ungodly.[8]

FAITH ALIVE

Would the world rather compromise Christians or oppose us actively? Why do you think so? Give an example of what you have in mind.

What happens to our organized worship and praise of God when all our group energies are directed at defending ourselves against unfair attacks? How do you think God wants us to respond in situations like this?

FOES OF WORSHIP NEVER GIVE UP

The order of Persian emperors went Cyrus the Great (550–530 B.C.), Cambyses (530–521 B.C.), Darius (521–486 B.C.), Ahasuerus, also known as Xerxes (486–465 B.C.), and Artaxerxes (464–422 B.C.). Temple construction was interrupted during the reign of Cyrus and resumed and ended in the time of Darius. The incidents in Ezra 4:6–23 represent typical hostility to the exilic community throughout this era even though they occurred after the temple was completed.

Ahasuerus (Xerxes) was the Persian emperor during whose reign Esther became queen. Much of Ahasuerus's energy was consumed by military actions against Greece. Even during his active rule, what action did the adversaries of the worship of the Lord take against the exiles in Jerusalem and Judah? (Ezra 4:6)

Artaxerxes was emperor when Ezra finally came to Jerusalem (Ezra 7:1–6) and when Nehemiah built Jerusalem's wall (Neh. 2:1–5). How many letters did the writer of the Book of Ezra have before him as evidence of the ongoing hostility of adversaries to the people of God during Artaxerxes' reign? (Ezra 4:7, 8)

How did Rehum and Shimshai try to make themselves and their opinions seem important to Artaxerxes? (Ezra 4:9, 10)

BEHIND THE SCENES

Osnapper is an Aramaic form of Ashurbanipal, the last great Assyrian emperor (669–633 B.C.), who is not generally associated with deportations to the area of Samaria. Around 640 B.C., Ashurbanipal did conquer Elam and the Persian capital of Shushan in the east while putting down extensive rebellions in the west. He may have swapped populations between Persia and Samaria then.[9]

What did Rehum and Shimshai have to say about the party of exiles Artaxerxes had authorized to return with Ezra? (Ezra 4:11, 12)

How did Rehum and Shimshai attempt to portray Jerusalem historically? (Ezra 4:13, 15)

How did Rehum and Shimshai present themselves in contrast to historical Jerusalem? (Ezra 4:14)

What did Rehum and Shimshai suggest would happen to Persia if Jerusalem was rebuilt? How realistic do you imagine this projection was? (Ezra 4:16)

 BEHIND THE SCENES

Persian emperors, along with most ancient monarchs, were illiterate. They dictated letters and decrees in Persian to scribes who translated them into Aramaic, the universal diplomatic language of the day. Once the documents arrived at their location, they were translated again from Aramaic into the local language. Correspondence coming to the emperors arrived in Aramaic and were translated by court scribes into Persian and then read aloud to the emperors.

How did Artaxerxes investigate the charge of Rehum and Shimshai against Jerusalem, and what did he discover? (Ezra 4:17–20)

What did Artaxerxes direct Rehum and Shimshai to do in his name? (Ezra 4:21, 22)

How did Rehum and Shimshai carry out Artaxerxes' order? How may they have overstepped their authority? (Ezra 4:23)

Ezra 4:24 resumes the story of the temple construction, last referred to in verse 5. What overall impressions of the local opposition to anything done by the Jews does Ezra 4:6–23 give you?

FAITH ALIVE

What can we as God's people do to overcome discouragement when unbelievers lie about us and create widely-accepted false impressions about us?

Instead of abandoning our worship, how should we emphasize it more when opponents of the Lord maintain organized opposition over long periods of time?

1. *Spirit-Filled Life® Bible* (Nashville: Thomas Nelson Publishers, 1991), 547, "Word Wealth, 2 Kin. 12:9, altar."
2. Ibid., 1017, "Word Wealth, Is. 42:21, law."
3. Ibid., 671, "Truth-in-Action through Ezra."
4. Ibid., 1360, "Word Wealth, Hab. 2:15, temple."
5. Ibid., 599, "Word Wealth, 1 Chr. 23:30, praise."
6. Ibid., 662, "Word Wealth, Ezra 3:11, great shout."
7. *Hayford's Bible Handbook* (Nashville: Thomas Nelson Publishers, 1995), 114, "Surveying Ezra," note on Ezra 3:10–13.
8. *Spirit-Filled Life® Bible,* 671, "Truth-in-Action through Ezra."
9. H. G. M. Williamson, *Ezra, Nehemiah,* Vol. 16 of *Word Biblical Commentary* (Waco, TX: Word Books, Publisher, 1985), 62.

Lesson 3/ Unstoppable Worship
Ezra 5—6

Princess Diana died in an automobile crash in Paris late in the summer of 1997. When people awoke that Sunday morning to the news of the tragedy the night before, a wave of sorrow swept across the western world that no one expected and no one can explain. Certainly, the print and electronic media sustained and glorified the mass mourning, but it did not create it. The movement to claim Diana as the "people's princess" arose spontaneously and took on a life of its own that defied easy analysis.

When the exiled Jews returned to Judah and Jerusalem from Babylon under the decree of Cyrus the Persian, they founded their fledgling province on the worship of the living God (Ezra 1:2–4; 3:1–7). Although the community faltered for sixteen years in the face of intense opposition from the people of Samaria (4:4, 5, 24), the spiritual forces of worship had been set in motion, and they could not be contained indefinitely. Neither could they be easily analyzed by human means. The Spirit of God was moving irresistibly behind the scenes.

THE POWER OF THE PROPHETIC ENTERPRISE

In the year 520 B.C., the second year of the Persian emperor Darius, the Holy Spirit raised up two prophets within the community of Judah and Jerusalem to revive the stalled project of rebuilding the temple of the Lord. None of the opponents of the people of the Lord knew it, but a powerful spiritual movement had begun.

Who were the two prophets who roused the Jews to resume building the temple of the Lord? (Ezra 5:1a)

By what authority did they deliver their messages to the residents of Judah and Jerusalem? (Ezra 5:1b)

Who were the key leaders who accepted the responsibility to overcome sixteen years of discouraged inertia and resume construction on the temple? (Ezra 3:2)

BIBLE EXTRA

Haggai was a plainspoken, motivational preacher; Zechariah was a visionary whose messages were intriguing and inspiring because they were puzzling. Together they delivered different aspects of the Word of the Lord.

What rebuke did the prophet Haggai hurl at the returned exiles because they had let opposition stop the temple construction? (Hag. 1:2–11)

Who did both prophets look to as the Lord's agent to get the temple built? (Hag. 2:4, 23; Zech. 4:6–10)

What special spiritual promises did the Lord make to His people through Haggai and Zechariah? (Hag. 2:5–9; Zech. 2:4, 5, 8; 3:1; 4:6, 10)

BEHIND THE SCENES

Judah, Samaria, Syria, Philistia, and other provinces were part of the fifth satrapy of Persia. Its name was "Beyond the River" (the Euphrates). Darius had organized Persia into twenty-three satrapies—large administrative units ruled by a governor called a satrap. Tattenai was a satrap. Shethar-Boznai was probably his investigator who handled serious complaints within the satrapy (Ezra 5:6).[1]

What did Tattenai the satrap and Shethar-Boznai his investigator want to know from Zerubbabel and Jeshua? (Ezra 5:3, 4)

Why didn't the investigation by Tattenai and Shethar-Boznai stop the temple construction as previous official inquiries had? (Ezra 5:5)

What might have concerned these officials when they saw a building of "heavy stones and timber" going up in an ancient city far away from the administrative centers of the empire? (Ezra 5:6–8)

Why do you imagine these officials were so careful to give a detailed account of their investigation of the Jews and the responses of the Jews to their inquiries? (Ezra 5:9–16)

What does the response of the Jews to Tattenai reveal about their insights into each of these topics?

• Their connection to the distant past (Ezra 5:1, 12)

• Their overall mission (Ezra 5:13–15)

• Their present task (Ezra 5:16)

What recommendation did Tattenai make to Darius the emperor based on his inquiry in Jerusalem? (Ezra 5:17)

When the surrounding peoples wrote to the emperors, what were their goals (see Ezra 4:4–8, 23)? How did the satrap's goal differ from those of the Jews' opponents?

 FAITH ALIVE

How should the ministry of God's preachers affect your motivation to do His will?

How should the ministry of God's preachers affect your ability to cope with opposition?

How can we distinguish between legitimate but annoying inquiries about our lives and ministries and hostile ones?

THE CONFIRMATION OF AN IMPERIAL DECREE

In Jerusalem Zerubbabel and Jeshua may have dreaded the prospect of hearing a response from the imperial court to Tattenai's inquiry. What they did not know was that the Lord was using the vast and intricate machinery of the Persian bureaucracy to guarantee the fulfillment of the prophetic words of Haggai and Zechariah.

Where did the search for Cyrus's decree authorizing the construction of the temple of the Lord in Jerusalem begin and end? (Ezra 6:1, 2)

 BEHIND THE SCENES

Achmetha is the Aramaic form of the name Ecbatana. Ecbatana was the ancient capital of Media (Ezra 3:2). Ecbatana was located nearly three hundred miles northeast of Babylon, high in the mountainous plateaus away from the Tigris-Euphrates plain. Cyrus the Great had spent the summer of 538 B.C. in Ecbatana to escape the heat of Shushan, his normal administrative center. He had issued his decree about Jerusalem in Ecbatana, and the official copy was still there.[2] The Persian Empire had four capital cities: Shushan (Susa), Ecbatana (Achmetha), Babylon, and Persepolis.

What did Darius discover that Cyrus the Great had decreed about the maximum allowable size of the temple and the involvement Persia should have in its construction? (Ezra 6:3–5)

What was Darius's basic instruction about how Tattenai the satrap of Beyond the River should relate to the building of the temple of the Lord in Jerusalem? (Ezra 6:6, 7)

What two things did Darius decree that his satrap should do for the Jews as they built the temple of the Lord without any outside interference?

1. (Ezra 6:8)

2. (Ezra 6:9)

What did Darius hope to gain from his benevolence toward the construction of the temple of the Lord in Jerusalem? (Ezra 6:10)

What penalties did Darius the Persian emperor attach to his edict authorizing the completion of the temple of the Lord in Jerusalem?

• Human sanctions (Ezra 6:11)

- Divine sanctions (Ezra 6:12)

What was the response of the satrap Tattenai, his investigator Shethar–Boznai, and the rest of the bureaucrats of Beyond the River to Darius's decree? (Ezra 6:13)

Underline the word "diligently" in Ezra 5:8; 6:12; and 6:13. What does this repetition indicate about God's involvement behind the scenes to see to it that His temple was completed?

 FAITH ALIVE

When have you seen the Lord work through secular human structures to accomplish His will or to advance His kingdom?

Why do you think the Lord chose to work through pagan emperors who had selfish reasons for the good they did and little, if any, appreciation of God's true glory and majesty?

In what sorts of situations do you think He might do something similar today?

THE JOY OF SACRIFICIAL COMMITMENT

In 538 B.C., when the exiles first returned from Babylon to Judah and Jerusalem, a spirit of sacrifice and commitment motivated them to begin constructing the temple. In 515 B.C., four and one-half years after Haggai and Zechariah jump-started the stalled temple project, the completion of the temple of the Lord in Jerusalem restored and renewed that original spirit of sacrifice and commitment. Success reignited the fires of faith that had brought the exiles home in the first place.

What roles did each of these play in the construction of the temple? (Ezra 6:14)

- The elders of Israel

- The prophets of God

- The God of Israel

- The emperors of Persia

BEHIND THE SCENES

The writer of the Book of Ezra listed Artaxerxes as one of the Persian emperors who played a role in building the temple (Ezra 6:14), even though his reign (464—422 B.C.) did not begin until much later. The author may have anticipated the partnership between Artaxerxes and both Ezra and Nehemiah in later reforms, or, more likely, he may have had in mind improvements made to the temple during Artaxerxes' reign that are not mentioned in the Bible (Ezra 7:27; 8:30).

BIBLE EXTRA

The month Adar (Ezra 6:15) was the last month of the year (roughly February-March in our solar calendar). The sixth year of Darius was 515 B.C. Solomon's temple had been destroyed by the Babylonian army of Nebuchadnezzar in July 586 B.C. (2 Kin. 25:1–4). How much time passed from July 586 B.C. to February-March 515 B.C.?

How long had the prophets of the Lord predicted the Babylonian captivity would last? (Jer. 25:11, 12; 29:10)

The time span of the temple's desolation best matches Jeremiah's seventy years. But, as mentioned in Lesson 1, what event do biblical writers look to as the end of the captivity? (2 Chr. 36:21–23; Ezra 1:1–4)

It may be that the Lord in His mercy shortened the seventy years of captivity. Even if the captivity started with the deportation of King Jehoiachin in 597 B.C. (2 Kin. 24:10–16) and ended with Cyrus's decree in 538 B.C., its duration was not quite sixty years.

Who joined in the celebration that marked the dedication of the temple of the Lord? (Ezra 6:16)

How did the lavish sacrifices offered at the dedication of the new temple compare with those offered when Solomon's temple was inaugurated? (Ezra 6:17; see 1 Kin. 8:62–64)

What else marked the dedication of Solomon's temple that did not occur when the second temple was consecrated? (2 Chr. 7:1–3)

In spite of their reduced circumstances and the absence of spectacular supernatural demonstrations, what was the dominant mood of the worshiping exiles as they dedicated the temple? (Ezra 6:16, 22)

Why do you suppose the exilic community offered twelve male goats as sin offerings for all the tribes of Israel when ten of the tribes had been destroyed, leaving just Judah and Benjamin? (Ezra 6:17)

Immediately following the dedication of the temple in the twelfth month (Ezra 6:15), the returned exiles celebrated the Passover in the first month (v. 19). Why were the priests and Levites ready to assist the worshipers with the slaughter of their Passover lambs? (Ezra 6:18, 20)

Who was eligible to participate in this first Passover celebrated after the temple of the Lord was completed? (Ezra 6:21)

The Passover marked the deliverance of Israel by the hand of the Lord from slavery in Egypt. What do you think this Passover celebration meant to these returned exiles who had suffered so much discouragement and opposition in the twenty-three years since they had come to their ancestral home?

Why do you think that, in this case, the writer of the Book of Ezra identifies the joy of the returned exiles as a joy specifically given them by the Lord? (Ezra 6:22)

 WORD WEALTH

Joy (Ezra 6:22) translates a Hebrew noun that denotes gladness and deep-seated merriness that penetrates the heart (Ps. 19:8) and soul (86:4) to the extent that it shows in one's eyes (Prov. 15:30). All sorts of things may give a person **joy**, from wine (Ps. 104:15) to weddings (Jer. 25:10), but the Lord and His salvation are the chief biblical reasons (Neh. 8:10; Ps. 5:11). The feasts of the Lord were primarily times of **joy** because at them the people of God came together to enjoy the Lord in one another's presence. This kind of group **joy** fortifies one's spirit for life and service.

FAITH ALIVE

When have you been part of a large group working for the Lord that stirred your spirit to renewed zeal for Him? How did the Lord work through that group experience for you?

In how many different ways have you found worship to be a source of deep and abiding joy?

In what area of your life would you like the Lord to make you joyful now? Write a brief prayer asking Him to make your heart, your soul, and your eyes glad in Him.

1. Edwin M. Yamauchi, "Ezra-Nehemiah," *The Expositor's Bible Commentary*, Vol. 4 (Grand Rapids: Zondervan Publishing House, 1988), 636.

2. Derek Kidner, *Ezra and Nehemiah: An Introduction and Commentary* (Leicester, England: InterVarsity Press, 1979), 56.

3. *Theological Wordbook of the Old Testament*, Vol. II (Chicago: Moody Press, 1980), 879.

Restoring and Renewing Repentance
(Ezra 7—10)

One hundred twenty-nine years after the first Jewish exiles returned to Judah and Jerusalem from Babylon, the priest and scribe Ezra led a second, much smaller contingent of Jews to strengthen the work of God among His people. Temple worship had been in effect for nearly sixty years by then. The Jewish community was once again deeply rooted in the soil of Palestine.

What did the Lord want of these believers who proudly bore His name among their pagan neighbors? He wanted a fresh sensitivity on their part to the beauty of holiness and the ugliness of sin. He wanted His people to have tender hearts, sensitive to the convicting voice of His Spirit. He wanted them to turn away quickly from what displeased Him.

So the Lord sent His people a messenger who had devoted his life to studying, obeying, and sharing the truth of His Word. Whenever our lives feel ineffective or stale, whenever we have experienced the chastening of the Lord, whenever we want to reach a greater level of intimacy with our Lord, one of our priorities must be repentance of sins revealed by the searchlight of God's Word. The Holy Spirit makes His dwelling and His base of operation in hearts quick to repent of sin.

Lesson 4/A Second Moses
Ezra 7—8

Her birthdate is uncertain—sometime around 1820. Her parents named her Araminta Ross, but everybody called her by her mother's name, Harriet. She was a slave in Maryland, even after she married John Tubman, a free man. Then she ran away to Philadelphia and vowed to spend her life getting others out of slavery.

During the decade before the Civil War, Harriet Tubman made eighteen forays back into Maryland and led out more than three hundred slaves—including her mother and father— through the Underground Railroad. She was in violation of the Fugitive Slave Act. Rewards for her capture totaled as much as $40,000.

During the war, Harriet Tubman served as nurse, scout, and spy for the Union Army. All the while she networked with slaves and friendly whites to help more black men, women, and children escape. In one military campaign alone, she helped more than 750 slaves get away. Black Americans, slave and free, called her Moses.[1]

Jewish tradition looked at Ezra as a second Moses too, but not because he led his people from bondage to freedom. Ancient rabbis revered the great biblical scribe for leading the Jews to revere the Law of God. Ezra was a second Moses for making his countrymen "people of the Book."

BORN TO LEAD A REVIVAL

Ezra finally appears in the seventh chapter of the book that bears his name. Chapters 7 through 9 are first-person memoirs of the great scribe Ezra. His personal narrative begins abruptly, as though no time had elapsed between the comple-

tion of the temple in 516 B.C. and the seventh year of Artaxerxes (458 B.C.). Then he lingers over his self-introduction,
consisting of the most extensive individual genealogy in the
Old Testament (7:1–5). Sixteen prominent names hit the high
spots of the millennium between Ezra and Aaron, the brother
of Moses and first priest of Israel.

 BIBLE EXTRA

> Several of Ezra's ancestors played important roles in
> earlier biblical history. Look up the following Bible passages
> and record the feats of some of his forebears.
>
> • Seraiah (Ezra 7:1; 2 Kin. 25:18–21; Jer. 52:24–27)
>
> • Hilkiah (Ezra 7:1; 2 Kin. 22:4–10; 23:4)
>
> • Zadok (Ezra 7:2; 1 Kin. 1:5–8, 38–40; 2:35)
>
> • Phinehas (Ezra 7:5; Num. 25:6–13)
>
> • Aaron (Ezra 7:5; Ex. 4:10–17; 32:1–6; Lev. 8—10)
>
> Only representative members of Ezra's ancestors
> appear in the genealogy in Ezra 7:1–5. For instance, since
> Seraiah was executed before the captivity, who entered
> Babylon to become Ezra's grandfather or great-grandfather?
> (1 Chr. 6:14, 15)

Springing from such a remarkable heritage, what sort of
man was this Ezra? (Ezra 7:6)

Look up the following verses and record your impression of how Ezra interpreted the successes he achieved. (Ezra 7:6, 9, 28; 8:18, 22, 31)

KINGDOM EXTRA

The hand of the Lord was upon him was a favorite expression of Ezra. "Hand" implies strength. The notion "upon him" notes that God's strength came and remained with Ezra. This abiding presence suggests an activity of the Holy Spirit. Ezra was not just a fortunate man, favored by God. He was the object of the Spirit's empowerment and enablement. Such empowerment for ministry falls under the New Testament terminology of the filling of the Holy Spirit (Acts 2:4; 4:8, 31). God's hand still rests on those He has called in Christ and commissioned to witness for His Son.

Who accompanied Ezra on his journey from Babylon to Jerusalem? (Ezra 7:7)

How long did it take Ezra and his companions to cover the eight hundred to nine hundred miles that separated Babylon and Jerusalem? (Ezra 7:8, 9)

How had Ezra prepared himself to be an incomparable tool in the hands of God among the people of Judah and Jerusalem? (Ezra 7:10)

FAITH ALIVE

Ezra was "a model reformer in that what he taught he had first lived, and what he lived he had first made sure of in the

Scriptures. . . . Study was saved from unreality, conduct from uncertainty, and teaching from insincerity and shallowness."[2]

If you were going to take just one step to become a better student of God's Word, what would it be?

If you were going to take just one step toward becoming a doer of the Word and not a hearer only (James 1:22), what would it be?

If you were going to take just one step toward becoming a more active teacher of God's Word, what would it be?

AUTHORIZED TO TEACH THE LAW

In the fifth official communication contained in the Book of Ezra, the emperor Artaxerxes gave his official stamp of approval to Ezra's ministry in Judah and Jerusalem. This remarkable document appears to have been written with the help of Jewish advisers because it reflects accurate knowledge of the levitical offerings and the personnel of the temple.

What was the Bible's assessment of Ezra and his qualifications for ministry? (Ezra 7:11)

What were Artaxerxes' assessments of himself and Ezra and their qualifications for their work? (Ezra 7:12)

- Of himself

- Of Ezra

Who did Artaxerxes authorize to move from Babylon to Jerusalem with Ezra? (Ezra 7:13)

What were the five specific tasks Artaxerxes committed to Ezra in his decree?

1. (Ezra 7:14)

2. (Ezra 7:15, 16)

3. (Ezra 7:17, 18)

4. (Ezra 7:19)

5. (Ezra 7:20)

What were Artaxerxes' instructions to the treasurers of the satrapy Beyond the River concerning Ezra and the temple of the Lord? (Ezra 7:21–24)

What judicial authority did Artaxerxes delegate to Ezra pertaining to the Jewish people because of his expertise in the Law of God? (Ezra 7:25, 26)

 KINGDOM EXTRA

Our faith that God is sovereign above all human authority allows the spirit of submission to prevail, because we know God can work through these authorities to accomplish His will. Accordingly, believe that God is able to work blessing for

His people through civil authority, even if it happens to be hostile. Trust His ability to work His will, even beyond civil government.[3]

For what did Ezra bless the Lord in relation to Artaxerxes and himself?

- In relation to Artaxerxes (Ezra 7:27)

- In relation to himself (Ezra 7:28a)

By what criterion did Ezra assemble the party of Jewish exiles that returned to Jerusalem with him? (Ezra 7:28b)

 FAITH ALIVE

For what aspects of the civil authorities you live under can you truly bless the Lord? Perhaps you should do so more often (1 Tim. 2:1–3).

For what mercies of God that have come to you through civil authorities can you truly bless God?

STAFFED TO REENERGIZE WORSHIP

Ezra had a commission from Artaxerxes to return to Judah and Jerusalem to strengthen the local worship of God and adherence to His Law. It was Persian policy to support the indigenous religions of all subject peoples in order to create stable, contented provinces. This gave Ezra the opportunity to handpick many of the people who went with him to achieve these ends that served both the empire and the Lord.

Who were the leaders of the two priestly families—the clan of Phinehas and the clan of Ithamar—represented in Ezra's entourage? (Ezra 8:2)

Who was the leader of the one royal family—the clan of David—represented in Ezra's company? (Ezra 8:2)

Each verse in Ezra 7:3–14 identifies a family of Judah or Benjamin that sent members to Jerusalem with Ezra. How many families were there?

What symbolic significance do you think this number might have?

Compare the families of Ezra's return (Ezra 7:3–14) with those of Jeshua and Zerubbabel's return 129 years earlier (2:3–15). How many of the families were represented in both groups of returning exiles?

Why do you suppose Ezra wanted relatives of people already in Judah and Jerusalem to be the ones who helped him challenge them to greater commitment to the Lord and His Law?

BEHIND THE SCENES

Neither Ahava (Ezra 8:15) nor Casiphia (v. 17) can be located from archaeological or historical evidence. It's likely that Ahava was both the name of a canal and a plain suitable for setting up a base camp.[4] It was probably south of the city of Babylon, since that is the area where most of the Jewish exiles were settled. Casiphia (which means "silver") would have been a nearby town. Some speculate it was another name for Ctesiphon, a city just north of Babylon.[5]

What did Ezra do to remedy the absence of any Levites from the company of exiles gathered at Ahava to return with him to Judah and Jerusalem? (Ezra 8:15–17)

BIBLE EXTRA

In many ways the congregation waiting to go to Jerusalem was like the children of Israel leaving Egypt for the Promised Land. Ezra was its Moses. The twelve family groupings paralleled the twelve tribes of Israel. And there were priests, but there were no Levites.

What role had the Levites played in the Exodus from Egypt to Canaan? (Num. 1:49–53)

What was Ezra taking from Babylon to Jerusalem that needed the attention of the Levites as the tabernacle had? (Ezra 7:15, 19; 8:24–30)

Who were the leaders of the Levites who responded to Ezra's appeal to go to Judah and Jerusalem, and how many of their kinsmen joined them? (Ezra 7:18, 19)

The Nethinim were menial temple servants—assistants to the Levites, as the Levites were assistants to the priests. Their genealogical lists always include Gentile names among the Jewish ones. How enthusiastic was their response to Ezra's (Ezra 8:20) appeal for help with the mission "to beautify the house of the LORD"? (Ezra 7:27)

Why is it that the poor and humble of God's people are often more responsive to His calls for sacrifice than the wealthy and privileged?

FAITH ALIVE

Which is an evidence of maturity and humility: trying to do everything on my own or recruiting gifted helpers to share the work? Why is this so?

Where did Ezra find his model for building a team of leaders and workers: the best Persian management theory or patterns provided by the biblical history of God's work among His people? How can we act similarly in our churches?

PROTECTED BY THE HAND OF GOD

It took Ezra three days to realize his company needed Levites. It then took eight days to locate Sherebiah, Hashabiah, and their levitical kinsmen. Finally, the eight hundred to nine hundred-mile trek consumed four months (minus the twelve days it took to finalize the group composition). It sounds so simple—a matter of days on a calendar. But the reality consisted of women, children, and tons of precious metals exposed to thieves and natural disasters along the caravan routes and imperial highways.

How did Ezra go about insuring the safety of his group (estimated to number about five thousand)? (Ezra 8:21, 23)

Why had Ezra decided against using his imperial authority (Ezra 8:21–23) to requisition protection for his party and its goods over the course of the journey? (Ezra 8:22)

KINGDOM EXTRA

Ezra's fast (Ezra 8:21) models a dependence upon God that releases Him to work on the people's behalf. Fasting is affirmed by Jesus as an accepted—if not expected—practice in the life of every believer (Matt. 9:14, 15). The fast, when understood as an expression of humble dependence, exerts significant force in spiritual warfare, leading to the fulfillment of the purposes of God.[6]

Fasting involves a sacrificial denial of nourishment—sometimes long, sometimes short—while turning one's attention to seeking God during that denial. Ezra's fast had three goals. First, the people petitioned God to lead them in a "right way." This was the *guidance* focus of their fast. Second, they petitioned God to protect their little ones. This was the *assistance* focus of their fast. Finally, they petitioned God to protect their possessions. This was the *substance* focus of their fast.[7]

Although Ezra depended on the Lord for physical safety, he took careful precautions to maintain the integrity and reputation of everyone involved with transporting the wealth entrusted to him. What steps did Ezra take to see that the temple treasure arrived intact?

- At the start of the journey (Ezra 8:24–27)

- At the end of the journey (Ezra 8:29)

How did Ezra motivate the priests and Levites to take extreme care of the temple treasure? (Ezra 8:28)

 KINGDOM EXTRA

Leaders, ask the Lord to send others to help you in your assigned place of ministry. Do not try to accomplish the job alone.

Leaders, employ corporate fasting when you undertake a major project or enter a significant season in your church's life. Be assured that God regards the self-humbling that accompanies prayer and fasting.

Leaders, pursue excellence in your stewardship of material things. Keep all financial dealings "in the light."[8]

Describe how precisely and exactly God guarded and guided Ezra's journey to a successful culmination. (Ezra 8:31–34)

How did Ezra's company of returned exiles celebrate their arrival in the country and city of their ancestors? (Ezra 8:35)

    WORD WEALTH

Sin offering (Ezra 8:35) translates an Aramaic noun based on one of the common words for "sin." Within the rich Semitic vocabulary for sin, one group of words means to twist or distort God's moral standard. Another means to rebel against His standard. This noun belongs to the group that means to fall short of God's moral law. In a few cases, this being one, the word for missing the moral mark refers to the sacrifice for that moral and spiritual shortcoming. Ezra and his fellow-travelers realized that, no matter how successful their journey under God's good hand, they still were sinners who needed atonement and forgiveness for their failings.

What was the final step Ezra took to set in motion all the terms of Artaxerxes' decree about strengthening the worship of the Lord and implementing the Law of God in the land? (Ezra 8:36)

FAITH ALIVE

What has been the most remarkable instance of the protection of God you have experienced?

How did you respond to Him at the time? How might you respond to Him now after more mature reflection on His goodness?

How should the kindness and mercy of God toward us make us more mindful of our sinfulness and need for His forgiveness?

1. "Tubman, Harriet," *The World Book Encyclopedia,* Vol. 19 (Chicago: Field Enterprises Educational Corporation, 1975), 392.

2. Derek Kidner, *Ezra and Nehemiah: An Introduction and Commentary* (Leicester, England: InterVarsity Press, 1979), 62.

3. *Spirit-Filled Life® Bible* (Nashville: Thomas Nelson Publishers, 1991), 671, 672, "Truth-in-Action through Ezra."

4. H. G. M. Williamson, *Ezra, Nehemiah,* Vol. 16 of *Word Biblical Commentary* (Waco, TX: Word Books, Publisher, 1985), 116.

5. Edwin M. Yamauchi, "Ezra-Nehemiah," *The Expositor's Bible Commentary,* Vol. 4 (Grand Rapids: Zondervan Publishing House, 1988), 658, 659.

6. *Hayford's Bible Handbook* (Nashville: Thomas Nelson Publishers, 1995), 115, note on Ezra 8:21.

7. *Spirit-Filled Life® Bible,* 668, "Kingdom Dynamics, Ezra 8:21–23, Fasting to Spiritual Breakthrough."

8. Ibid., 672, "Truth-in-Action through Ezra."

9. *Theological Wordbook of the Old Testament,* Vol. I (Chicago: Moody Press, 1980), 277, 278.

Lesson 5/*The Horror of Sin*
Ezra 9—10

He had grown up in a Bible-believing church but wanted some freedom. Soon he found himself experimenting with drugs and alcohol along with his new friends. He knew it was wrong, and he kept expecting God to strike him down with a lightning bolt of judgment. But nothing dramatic happened to him. He dropped most of his contact with his parents and took a cheap apartment in a nasty part of town.

Then he moved in with a girl. She was pretty and willing and made him feel important. But he didn't love her and resented any suggestions that they get married. Now he really thought God was going to get him. He interpreted most comments anyone from his past made as criticisms of his lifestyle. He grew increasingly angry and suspicious.

Then the girl got pregnant and he wondered if she did it on purpose to trap him. He married her for the baby's sake, but now he hated her. They moved to a nicer apartment and started going into debt. He drank more, missed work more, and got fired. The only good thing he could see in it all was that God hadn't judged him. But then one day it occurred to him that judgment was built into the sin. He was living in hell.

RECOGNIZING THE RUIN SIN CAUSES

Whatever the priest-scribe Ezra expected to find when he and his company from Babylon arrived in Jerusalem, it wasn't the situation that arose to confront them. Probably Ezra anticipated a life as a scholar and educator. Instead he had to act as a hard-nosed problem solver. Initially he was almost overwhelmed.

How much time passed between Ezra's arrival in Jerusalem and the time when an ugly problem reared its head? (compare Ezra 10:9 with 7:9)

What was the moral-spiritual problem that was reported to Ezra? (Ezra 9:1, 2)

Who made the charge, and who were the ones primarily involved in the offense? (Ezra 9:1, 2)

 BIBLE EXTRA

Ezra 9:1 lists eight people-groups of the ancient Near East. Only the Ammonites, Moabites, and Egyptians still existed in the days of Ezra.[1] Look up Exodus 34:11–16; Leviticus 18:3; Deuteronomy 7:1–4; 23:3; summarize why these old names were the ones on the minds of the concerned leaders of the Jews.

 WORD WEALTH

Trespass (Ezra 9:2) translates a Hebrew noun meaning "unfaithfulness." The sin connected to intermarriage was not so much the violation of a statute or commandment as much as it was an offense against the relationship the children of Israel had formed with the Lord by entering a covenant with Him at Mount Sinai.[2] They were a "holy seed" (Ezra 9:2), not because they were racially superior to anyone, but because they belonged to the Lord. Any Gentile who turned to the Lord was welcomed into Israel, but pagans could not be. The issue throughout this passage is **trespass** as unfaithfulness to the Lord rather than as lawbreaking.

What was Ezra's reaction to the news that various leaders of the Jews had married pagan wives? (Ezra 9:3–5a)

What was the response of those who observed Ezra's grief? (Ezra 9:4)

The evening sacrifice occurred at 3:00 P.M. Ezra probably had mourned for several hours by then. What was his next step of response to the unfaithfulness of the priests and noblemen? (Ezra 9:5)

KINGDOM EXTRA

When Ezra fell on his knees and spread out his hands to the Lord (Ezra 9:5), he exemplified the kind of intercession that can inspire confidence for us as believers in contemporary circumstances. Remembering that to intercede is to come before God on behalf of someone else, we can effect change in the spiritual realm. When we believe that God hears and answers the prayers of His church, we will exercise this kingdom privilege more and more effectively.[3]

FAITH ALIVE

What changes in your perspective on sin when you look at it as unfaithfulness to God rather than the breaking of a rule?

We live in a society that prides itself on being unshockable by immorality and violence. We have turned one into an alternative lifestyle and both into entertainment. How can we sensitize our spirits to sin so that sin still astonishes us with its ugliness? (Rom. 12:9; Eph. 5:1–12)

When has sin grieved you so that you were moved to physical expressions of sorrow and shame? What did you learn from that experience?

CONFESSING THE REBELLION AT SIN'S ROOT

When Ezra mourned over the intermarriage of Jewish leaders with pagan women from the surrounding nations, he tore his clothes, pulled out his hair, and sat in stunned silence. Singly, each of these was a mark of sorrow. Together they indicated mourning for the dead.[4] Ezra's grief was extreme; his posture in prayer indicated abject humility before God. His words revealed the pain in his heart.

Why was Ezra "ashamed and humiliated" as he knelt before the Lord and stretched out his hands to Him? (Ezra 9:6)

How did the sin of the returned exiles relate to the long history of national sin that had led to captivity and exile? (Ezra 9:7)

 WORD WEALTH

Iniquities (Ezra 9:6) translates the Hebrew noun derived from a verb "to bend" or "to distort." Thus **iniquity** is the "evil bent" within human beings or the "crooked" direction or "warped" deeds of sinners. The first mention of **iniquity** in the Bible is in Genesis 4:13, where Cain finally understood the enormity of his deed and stated: "My punishment [iniquity] is greater than I can bear." Knowing that **iniquity** is something too heavy to be borne by fallen humanity, God promised that His Suffering Servant would bear the **iniquities** of His people (Is. 53:11).[5]

How did Ezra view the eighty years between the decree of Cyrus in 538 B.C. and his own time in 458 B.C.? (Ezra 9:8)

How had God extended mercy to the remnant of the captivity through the emperors of Persia? (Ezra 9:9)

What commands given through the prophets (including Moses) had Israel historically ignored?

- Concerning the land (Ezra 9:11)

- Concerning intermarriage with pagans (Ezra 9:12)

 WORD WEALTH

Peace (Ezra 9:12) translates the Hebrew noun *shalom*. *Shalom* comes from the root verb *shalam*, meaning "to be complete, perfect, and full." Thus *shalom* is much more than the absence of war and conflict; it is the wholeness that the entire human race seeks.

The word *shalom* occurs about 250 times in the Old Testament. In Psalm 35:27, God takes delight in the *shalom* (the wholeness, the total well-being) of His servant. In Isaiah 53:5, the chastisement necessary to bring us *shalom* was upon the suffering Messiah. The angels understood at His birth that Jesus was to be the great peace-bringer, as they called out, "Glory to God in the highest: and on earth **peace**, goodwill toward men!" (Luke 2:14–17; compare Is. 9:7). The pagans around God's people in Ezra's day could never know this **peace** without turning to the Lord in trust and obedience.[6]

What features of their present dilemma struck Ezra as being incredible? (Ezra 9:13, 14)

As Ezra considered the Lord God of Israel and the remnant from the captivity, how did their characters contrast with one another? (Ezra 9:15)

KINGDOM EXTRA

A servant leader asks God's people to do what he himself has established in his own life. This should first be evident in the way he deals with sin and be manifest in his spirit of repentance.

Leaders, choose to intercede for God's people rather than become upset with them. Identify with their sin and confess it as your own. Leaders, learn to lead in the confession of sin as a model for your people.[7]

FAITH ALIVE

What would happen to the spiritual life of your church if every member stopped being critical of other members and began to be personally concerned about and to accept some responsibility for their sins?

In what ways do Christians today sometimes presume on the kindness and mercy of God while repeating selfish acts of unfaithfulness just as the Jews did in Ezra's day?

How would it affect the way you confess sin and pray for forgiveness if you focused more on the righteous character of the Lord to whom you are confessing?

ACTING BECAUSE OF REPENTANCE

Ezra had been granted extensive authority by the Persian emperor Artaxerxes to enforce the Law of God (Ezra 7:25, 26). When the time came for him to act in response to lawlessness on the part of the Jews, however, Ezra's first inclination was not to rush about issuing legal rulings and imposing penalties. For Ezra, to act meant to seek the face of the Lord.

Where was Ezra when he poured out his heart in confession to God about the sins of the Jews? (Ezra 9:5—10:1)

What physical actions accompanied Ezra's hours-long prayer of grief, mourning, and confession? (Ezra 9:5; 10:1)

What impact did Ezra's intensely spiritual and physical prayer of repentance have on the segment of the Jewish community that cared about the will of the Lord? (Ezra 10:1)

What did Shechaniah of the clan of Elam (Ezra 2:7; 8:7) have to say as the spokesman for the people who confessed with Ezra about each of these?

- The problem facing the Jews (Ezra 10:2)

- A solution to that problem (Ezra 10:3)

- Ezra's role in that solution (Ezra 10:4)

    KINGDOM EXTRA

We must be careful lest we forget the cost of forgiveness. Sin is serious, and we must deal with it seriously! Sin sent God's only Son to the Cross. Let us not forget that God's conditions for forgiveness include our repentance, confession, and forsaking of our sins.

Take sin seriously, and deal with it thoroughly. Follow through with repentance. Take steps to right the wrongs sin has brought about. Do not pervert forgiveness by continuing in sin.[8]

What did Ezra feel was the best way to guarantee that what people said in the heat of emotion would get done after they had time to think about things? (Ezra 10:5)

WORD WEALTH

Swear an oath (Ezra 10:5) translates a Hebrew verb meaning "to swear," "to give one's word," or "to bind oneself with an oath." The origin of the verb appears to be the Hebrew noun for "seven." To **swear an oath** literally meant "to seven oneself," that is, to repeat some detail of the oath seven times. In Genesis 21:28–31, Abraham gave seven lambs to Abimelech when entering an agreement with him. The seven lambs witnessed that Abraham had dug a well, which was named Beersheba. Beersheba meant either "Well of the Oath" or "Well of the Seven."[9] To swear an oath obligated an Israelite by his sacred, unbreakable word to perform an action or refrain from an action.[10] In this context, the leaders of the Jews bound themselves to do what they had promised Ezra.

What did Ezra do while the priests and elders put out a proclamation to the residents of Judah and Jerusalem? (Ezra 10:6)

What were the terms of the proclamation that went throughout Judah, and what were the penalties for disobeying it? (Ezra 10:7, 8; see 7:26)

What was the situation of the assembly that gathered to deal with the problem of Jews intermarrying with pagan women? (Ezra 10:9)

BEHIND THE SCENES

In 458 B.C., the twentieth day of the ninth month (Kislev) was well into December. The rainy season had begun in October; its heaviest rains would have fallen in December and January. The temperature high might have reached 50 degrees Fahrenheit. The crowd gathered in the open square suffered both physical discomfort and spiritual turmoil.

What was Ezra's instruction to the assembly of all the men of Judah and Benjamin? (Ezra 10:10, 11)

What was the response of the assembly of the men of Judah and Benjamin to the verdict of Ezra?

- Their general response (Ezra 10:12)

- Their conditional responses (Ezra 10:13)

- Their detailed proposal (Ezra 10:14)

Why do you think Ezra allowed others to play such a large part in solving the problem of intermarrying with pagans (Ezra 10:2–4, 12–14)? Does this seem wise or wishy-washy to you? Why?

Do you think the opponents to the plan for dealing with intermarrying with pagan wives were "doves" who didn't want to punish the sinners or "hawks" who didn't want to delay the punishment until the committee could evaluate each case? Why did you reach this conclusion? (Ezra 10:15)

FAITH ALIVE

When a major problem arises in your life, what tends to be your characteristic way of reacting to it? Circle the letter of the item that best describes your probable response.

   a. Get depressed.

   b. Act first; think later.

   c. Pray.

   d. Formulate a plan of action.

   e. Talk it over with friends.

   f. Other

_____

_____

What do you observe about the way Ezra approached the problem of intermarriage with pagans that might help you respond better to problems in the future?

What does repentance of our sins do to our perspective on life that makes it easier for us to know how to deal with the consequences of those sins?

IF YOUR EYE OFFENDS YOU, PLUCK IT OUT

The prophet Malachi, perhaps a contemporary of Ezra, tells us that God hates divorce (Mal. 2:16). It's surprising to find the chief teacher of the Law of God leading God's people into divorce proceedings. What Ezra did set no precedent for anyone looking for an excuse to get a divorce. A uniquely dangerous situation called for a uniquely harsh solution.

Who formed the review commission responsible for evaluating each case of intermarriage between the Jews and pagans? (Ezra 10:16)

How long did it take the committee to complete its work of reviewing each case of intermarriage between Jewish men and pagan wives? (Ezra 10:16, 17)

Who was identified first as sinning against God's Law by marrying a pagan wife from the surrounding nations? (Ezra 10:18; see 3:2, 8; 4:3; 5:2)

What pattern of response to the ruling of the examining committee that they were guilty did the priestly offenders establish for the rest of the Jews? (Ezra 10:19)

What was the total number of priests found guilty of intermarrying with pagan wives? (Ezra 10:18–22)

How many Levites in various kinds of temple service had intermarried? (Ezra 10:23, 24)

How many ordinary members of Judah and Benjamin had married pagan wives? (Ezra 10:25–43)

What made many of these divorces more painful than the others? (Ezra 10:44)

 BEHIND THE SCENES

Divorce had become unfortunately common among the postexilic community in Judah and Jerusalem. Many Jewish men had divorced their wives in order to marry wealthy pagan women (Mal. 2:10–16). Rabbinic tradition said these divorces occurred because the Jewish women had lost their beauty toiling in the sun to rebuild their homes and farms.[11] The divorces Ezra ordered, although not up to the standards of Jesus (Matt. 19:3–10) and the New Testament (1 Cor. 7:12–16), were an appropriate one-time response to a horrible situation.

 ### KINGDOM EXTRA

The Jews of Ezra's day who intermarried with pagans had forgotten that when two people marry, God stands as a witness to the marriage. He seals it with the strongest possible word: *covenant.* "Covenant" speaks of faithfulness and enduring commitment. It stands like a divine sentinel over marriage, for blessing or for judgment.

In Malachi 2:16, divorce is described as *violence.* To initiate divorce does violence to God's intention for marriage and to the mate to whom one has been joined.

Yet where husband and wife live together according to their marriage vows, all the power of a covenant-keeping God stands behind them and their marriage. What a confidence, to know that *God backs up our marriage.* His power and authority stand against every enemy that would violently threaten it from without or within.[12]

 ### FAITH ALIVE

What kinds of sins do you think Christians need to dread as threats to our spiritual health as deadly as marriage to pagans was to the Jews?

Jesus taught us to deal ruthlessly with our sins when we become aware of them (Matt. 5:29, 30). Identify a sin you have had trouble eliminating from your thought or behavior pattern. How could you deal ruthlessly with this sin? (Could another hold you accountable? Do you need to make restitution?)

1. Edwin M. Yamauchi, "Ezra-Nehemiah," *The Expositor's Bible Commentary,* Vol. 4 (Grand Rapids: Zondervan Publishing House, 1988), 662.

2. H. G. M. Williamson, *Ezra, Nehemiah,* Vol. 16 of *Word Biblical Commentary* (Waco, TX: Word Books, Publisher, 1985), 132.

3. *Hayford's Bible Handbook* (Nashville: Thomas Nelson Publishers, 1995), 115, note on Ezra 9:5.

4. Williamson, *Ezra, Nehemiah,* 132, 133.

5. *Spirit-Filled Life® Bible* (Nashville: Thomas Nelson Publishers, 1991), 867, "Word Wealth, Ps. 130:3, iniquities."

6. Ibid., 1334, "Word Wealth, Nahum 1:15, peace."

7. Ibid., 672, "Truth-in-Action through Ezra."

8. Ibid., 671.

9. Ibid, 42, 43, "Word Wealth, Gen. 26:3, swore."

10. *Theological Wordbook of the Old Testament,* Vol. II (Chicago: Moody Press, 1980), 900.

11. Yamauchi, "Ezra-Nehemiah," *The Expositor's Bible Commentary,* Vol. 4, 677.

Restoring and
Renewing Security
(Nehemiah 1:1—7:3)

In the Book of Ezra, God's concern was restoring the temple and renewing the commitment of His people to His Law. In the Book of Nehemiah, God's concern is restoring the walls of Jerusalem and renewing His covenant with His people. The history and geography of these two books provide an interesting and helpful parallel to the restoring and renewing work of God in our lives.

First, central to the city and central to worship, the temple can be likened to *the human spirit*. Sin destroys our relationship with God and our capacity to worship Him. Rebirth in Christ (a reconstructed temple) makes renewed worship and fellowship with God a living possibility.

Second, central to the rule of the surrounding land or territory, the city can be likened to *the human soul*. Just as the walls and gates had been ruined by sin's judgment, so the impact of sin in the personality deteriorates the human capacity to will to live under God's will and rule.

Third, the environs are intended to be a land of peace and fruitful harvest and can be likened to the *human body*. Through it, God may channel and manifest His kingdom witness or it might manifest actions that contradict or violate God's purposes.[1]

Whenever our lives feel ineffective or stale, whenever we have experienced the chastening of the Lord, whenever we want to reach a greater level of intimacy with our Lord, one of our priorities must be letting God's Spirit rebuild our souls and personalities. The Holy Spirit makes His dwelling and His base of operation in hearts secure in His power.

Lesson 6/A Man with a Mission
Nehemiah 1—2

Albert Ball wanted to be an aviator in the Royal Flying Corps during World War I. He paid for his own military flight instruction at Hendon Field, where he wrecked several trainer planes and barely passed his solo flight. The Royal Flying Corps assigned him to fly a lumbering reconnaissance plane as an artillery spotter. He ignored his duties and crossed the lines looking for German planes to shoot at with his rifle.

The Corps transferred Ball to fighters and he soon racked up thirty kills—the most by a British pilot. Ball was obsessed. He chased multiple enemy planes alone. He flew head-on at German planes, firing only when collision seemed inevitable. He dared enemy fighters to pull in behind him so he could suddenly drop below them and rise on their tails.

Ball seemed invincible. He lived apart from the other pilots, accompanied by his violin and Kipling's poetry. When he started fearing death, he left the front lines to be a flight instructor. He couldn't stand the boredom and returned to action. Nothing mattered to him but aerial combat. With forty-two confirmed kills to his credit, Albert Ball went down on May 7, 1917, before the guns of Lothar von Richtofen, the younger brother of the famed Red Baron.[2]

Captain Albert Ball, Britain's greatest air ace of the Great War, was a man with a mission. Nothing satisfied him apart from that mission. It eventually destroyed him.

Nehemiah also was a man with a mission that defined him as thoroughly as Albert Ball's defined him. But Nehemiah's mission did not destroy him. It gave his life great meaning and purpose.

A MISSION BASED ON NEED AND PRAYER

Unlike the meditative, scholarly Ezra, Nehemiah was a man of action. However, he was a godly man of action. He knew when to wait on God. He knew that waiting on God was never wasting time; it was preparing his heart and getting his marching orders.

What does the opening chapter of the Book of Nehemiah tell us about this man?

- Who (Neh. 1:1, 2)

- What (Neh. 1:11b)

- Where (Neh. 1:1)

- When (Neh. 1:1; 2:1)

 WORD WEALTH

The name **Nehemiah** (Neh. 1:1) means "The Consolation of God" and derives from the Hebrew verb *nacham* (to breathe strongly, to pity, to console) and from *Yah,* the sacred name of the Lord. In short, **Nehemiah** means "the consoling breath or spirit of God." It implies "pity that becomes active in the interest of another." Nehemiah begins to appear as a picture of the Holy Spirit, with a name virtually synonymous with His. Not surprisingly, Nehemiah's ministry gives us a photograph of God's Spirit assisting us in the recovery of those ruined parts of our lives sin has disintegrated.[3]

What two concerns did Nehemiah question his brother Hanani about? (Neh. 1:2)

What did Hanani tell Nehemiah about each of the concerns he had inquired about? (Neh. 1:3)

What was Nehemiah's response to the information his brother Hanani gave him? (Neh. 1:4)

BEHIND THE SCENES

The twentieth year of Artaxerxes was 445 B.C. Thirteen years had passed since Ezra's mission to Jerusalem (458 B.C.). Roughly seventy years had passed since the temple was completed under the ministry of Haggai and Zechariah (516 B.C.). More than ninety years had passed since the first exiles had returned with Jeshua the priest and Zerubbabel (538 B.C.). One hundred forty years had passed since the Babylonian army under Nebuchadnezzar had destroyed the walls of Jerusalem (586 B.C.).

Nehemiah would not have been distraught over news of the Babylonian destruction of the walls and gates. What he heard for the first time was that preliminary wall and gate construction done after the return of Ezra had recently been demolished by neighboring opponents (see Ezra 4:7–23).

Describe the following aspects of Nehemiah's prayer.

- His description of God (Neh. 1:5)

- His general appeal (Neh. 1:6a)

- The overall nature of his prayer (Neh. 1:6b)

- His admission (Neh. 1:7)

- His case from Scripture (Neh. 1:8, 9)

- His petition for the Jews (Neh. 1:10)

- His petition for himself (Neh. 1:11)

WORD WEALTH

Two Hebrew nouns are translated "mercy" in Nehemiah's prayer. The first is *hesed* (Neh. 1:5), which refers to the Lord's loyal love toward those who enter His covenant. The second is *rahamim* (Neh. 1:11), which denotes the tender compassion of the Lord toward His servants. We, like Nehemiah, can approach God in prayer only because of the merciful covenant relationship He has extended to us. Within that covenant relationship we, like Nehemiah, can appeal to the compassionate heart of the Lord about our particular requests and concerns.

KINGDOM EXTRA

If you want to see your personality rebuilt around your redeemed spirit as Nehemiah wanted to see the walls of Jerusalem rebuilt around the temple of the Lord, that rebuilding must be undertaken from a stance on your knees. The Holy Spirit will assist you. Just as Nehemiah's prayer shows us how to confess and pray from the promises of God's Word, so the Spirit will help your weaknesses when you do not know how to pray as you should (Rom. 8:26, 27).

The building process involves your partnership with the Spirit, and prayer is the meeting point of that partnering. He will not do the job for you but is present to accomplish the task through you and in you. Daily "executive planning sessions" will advance the project.[4]

 ## FAITH ALIVE

How do you sense a need for the Holy Spirit to rebuild the walls of your mind? For instance, do you struggle with doubts, impure thoughts, or an inability to focus?

How do you sense a need for the Holy Spirit to rebuild the walls of your emotions? For instance, do fear, lust, anger, or unforgiveness hinder your spiritual growth?

How do you sense a need for the Holy Spirit to rebuild the walls of your will? For instance, do you need confidence, resistance, or the ability to move ahead?[5]

A MISSION BASED ON PAST FAITHFULNESS

Through an extended period of prayer and fasting (Neh. 1:4), Nehemiah received a sense of mission and calling to rebuild the walls of Jerusalem. But he was not free to come and go as he chose. His every move was subject to the approval of the Persian emperor Artaxerxes. Nehemiah's future depended on how well his past service inclined the emperor to favor him.

Four months had passed between the ninth month Chislev (Neh. 1:1) and the first month Nisan (2:1). What momentous occasion marked the resumption of Nehemiah's story in the month Nisan? (Neh. 2:1)

What breach of court etiquette was Nehemiah guilty of, and what was his reaction when it was brought to his attention? (Neh. 2:1, 2)

What differences can you observe between the manner in which the mighty emperor talks to his servant and the way Nehemiah talks to Artaxerxes? (Neh. 2:2–6)

Once Nehemiah could see that Artaxerxes was favorable to the mission the Lord had put in his heart during four months of prayer and fasting, how did his confidence in God's leading show in the way he spoke to the emperor? (Neh. 2:7, 8)

 KINGDOM EXTRA

Nehemiah wanted to see his homeland made whole: the Lord enthroned in His temple, surrounded by protecting walls, situated in the middle of Judah enjoying peace. This kind of wholeness is reflected in the concept of "holiness." What the *Holy* Spirit is up to is to bring the *whole* life of Jesus Christ into the *whole* of our personalities so the *whole* love of God can be relayed to the *whole* world.[6]

If there is anything that summarizes the meaning of the Holy Spirit's mission to earth, it is His reflection of the Father's desire that everyone come to know the life and the love He has opened for the whole world to share. Though it is God's holiness that man has violated, it is also His holiness—His very *Spirit* of holiness—that He has sent into the world. His holy purpose is to restore—to rebuild wholly—just as Nehemiah's concern was for complete construction.[7]

What kinds of authority was Nehemiah armed with when he traveled from the citadel at Shushan in Persia to the satrapy "Beyond the River," of which Judah was a small part? (Neh. 2:8c, 9)

What was the reaction to Nehemiah's letters by at least some of the officials in the provinces around Judah within the satrapy "Beyond the River"? (Neh. 2:10)

BEHIND THE SCENES

Sanballat's name (Neh. 2:10) was Babylonian, built around Sin the moon god. He was probably from Upper or Lower Beth Horon, two villages about twelve miles northwest of Jerusalem on the main road to the Mediterranean coast. He was a leader of the Samarian opposition. Tobiah was a Jewish name meaning "The Lord Is Good." He probably was a worldly Jew living in and controlling the territory associated with Ammon east of the Jordan River. These two men would be Nehemiah's bitter enemies for years to come.[8]

FAITH ALIVE

Nehemiah had imperial authority to restore and renew the walls of Jerusalem (Neh. 2:8). The Holy Spirit enters the life of every believer in Christ with divine authority to restore and renew it. What aspect(s) of your mind, emotions, and/or will that you identified earlier as needing repair would you like Him to work on right away?

Nehemiah was authorized to get timbers from the king's forest (Neh. 2:8). The rest of his building materials were usable stones among the rubble of Jerusalem. As the Holy Spirit restores your mind, emotions, and will, what do you think He will bring to the task directly from the Lord and what will He use from your personality that you might be inclined to call junk?[9]

A MISSION BASED ON CAREFUL PREPARATION

While he had been in the Persian court, Nehemiah was on familiar ground. Once he arrived in Judah—the native country he had never seen—Nehemiah had to do careful research in order to understand the situation and the people involved.

Three days seemed to be a normal time to recover from the journey between Mesopotamia and Judah (Neh. 2:11; see Ezra 8:32). What things may Nehemiah have learned during those three days about the situation in Jerusalem and Judah that he profited from later? (Neh. 2:10; 5:3, 4; 6:18)

How did Nehemiah size up the scope of the wall rebuilding project without arousing the curiosity of the local leaders or residents? (Neh. 2:12–15)

What did Nehemiah discover on his reconnaissance mission around the southern and eastern portions of the wall? (Neh. 2:13–15)

The leaders and residents of Jerusalem and Judah had experienced seventy-one years of frustrating opposition from their neighbors since the temple of the Lord had been completed in 516 B.C. Their recent building project failure (Ezra 4:11, 12, 23) was fresh in their minds. What negative reactions from the leaders and people may Nehemiah have avoided by keeping his mission secret until he gathered the information he needed? (Neh. 2:12, 16)

When Nehemiah finally assembled the people of Jerusalem and Judah to reveal his plan to them, what motivational value would each of these factors have had?

1. Their current reproach (Neh. 2:17)

2. God's intervention for Nehemiah (Neh. 2:18a)

3. Authorization by Artaxerxes (Neh. 2:18b)

How do you think Sanballat, Tobiah, and Geshem hoped to discourage Nehemiah and the Jews with each of these tactics? (Neh. 2:19)

1. Laughter and derision

2. Accusation of rebellion

 BEHIND THE SCENES

Extrabiblical sources reveal that Geshem (Neh. 2:19) led an assortment of Arab tribes that controlled the deserts south of Judah from Egypt to the Arabian peninsula. He was more powerful than Sanballat and Tobiah combined, but his hostility to the Jews appears to have been less intense. Sanballat to the north, Tobiah to the east, and Geshem to the south forged a hostile boundary around Nehemiah and Judah.[10]

 KINGDOM EXTRA

The mocking, accusing confrontation of Sanballat, Tobiah, and Geshem portrays the predictable method of satanic opposition to the rebuilding work of the Holy Spirit in your personality. It is always hurled at you when hope is rising. As soon as you believe God is *really* going to work something beautiful in your life and as soon as you respond with a will to partner with His purpose, Satan the accuser will scream, "You have no right to even *think* of that. Don't you realize your past life has removed your right to expect God's blessing? You've rebelled against the King in the past. You're dreaming!"

But the Holy Spirit will stand by you, just as Nehemiah rose to declare to Sanballat, "The God of heaven Himself will prosper us; therefore we His servants will arise and build" (Neh. 2:20).[11]

Nehemiah categorically rejected the right of Sanballat, Tobiah, and Geshem to comment on the divinely inspired rebuilding of the walls of Jerusalem. How did he dismiss them from any claim on Jerusalem? (Neh. 2:20)

- Past ("no heritage")

- Present ("no right")

- Future ("no memorial")

 KINGDOM EXTRA

When Nehemiah denied the enemies of the Jews any heritage, right, or memorial in Jerusalem (Neh. 2:20), he demonstrated a significant principle for anyone engaged in spiritual warfare. The powers of darkness who would oppose God's rebuilding program—physical or spiritual—have no legal right—past, present, or future—within God's kingdom (see Col. 2:13–15). Declaring this in prayer becomes a powerful instrument against the Adversary.[12]

 FAITH ALIVE

Nehemiah identified with the distress the Jews of Jerusalem had been living with for years (Neh. 2:17). How does the Lord through His Holy Spirit identify with the distress you feel over the broken area(s) of your life that you have identified in this lesson?

Nehemiah committed himself to build alongside the Jews who had lived in distress if they too would commit themselves to the task (Neh. 2:17). What assurance do you have from God's Word that the Holy Spirit is committed to remaking your life after the likeness of the Lord Jesus?

Nehemiah pledged himself to become a companion of the builders of Jerusalem's walls (Neh. 2:17). What kind of partnership in rebuilding your life can you expect if the Holy Spirit wants to be your companion?[13]

1. Jack W. Hayford, *Rebuilding the Real You* (Ventura, CA: Regal Books, 1986), 58, 59.

2. Melissa Newland, "Britain's First Air Ace," *British Heritage* (October/November 1997), 17–19.

3. Hayford, *Rebuilding the Real You*, 36, 37.

4. Ibid., 75.

5. Ibid., 63, 64.

6. Ibid., 80.

7. Ibid., 82.

8. Edwin M. Yamauchi, "Ezra-Nehemiah," *The Expositor's Bible Commentary*, Vol. 4 (Grand Rapids: Zondervan Publishing House, 1988), 687, 688.

9. Hayford, *Rebuilding the Real You*, 105–108.

10. Yamauchi, "Ezra-Nehemiah," *The Expositor's Bible Commentary*, Vol. 4, 691.

11. Hayford, *Rebuilding the Real You*, 159, 160.

12. *Hayford's Bible Handbook* (Nashville: Thomas Nelson Publishers, 1995), 120, note on Neh. 2:20.

13. Hayford, *Rebuilding the Real You*, 155.

Lesson 7/A Man with a Plan
Nehemiah 3—4

The single-minded businessman always had a plan. To recharge his batteries after eighty-hour work weeks, he built a cottage on a distant lake as a weekend retreat. To make his plan more efficient, he learned to fly and kept an old car for weekend transport at the airfield nearest his lake.

After a while, the businessman further fine-tuned his plan by fitting his plane with pontoons so he could land on the lake and taxi right up to his pier. On his first trip in the newly-rigged plane, he flew by force of habit straight to the rural airport, where he started his descent.

"What are you doing? There aren't any wheels on this thing," his wife screamed, just in time for our businessman with a plan to pull up before touching down. Somewhat shaken, he flew on to the lake and made a perfect landing. As the plane drifted to a stop at the pier, he turned sheepishly to his wife and said, "I'm sorry, dear. I should have planned more carefully and built in reminders about the change in flight plans. I won't let it happen again."

Then he opened his door and hopped confidently out of the plane into eight feet of water.

Some plans are better than others. Some planners are better than others. God entrusted the mission of rebuilding the walls of Jerusalem to Nehemiah because he was among the best planners—creative, decisive, flexible, and passionate about God and His people.

MOBILIZING THE MASSES

There may have been several leaders in Jerusalem who could have motivated the populace to take on the project of

Nehemiah's Jerusalem.[1]

Wall Builders

NEHEMIAH'S JERUSALEM

Sheep

Fish

Old

Miphkad

East

Horse

Temple

Ophel

3
2
1
32
31
30
30
29
29
28

4
4
5
5
6
7
8
8
9
10

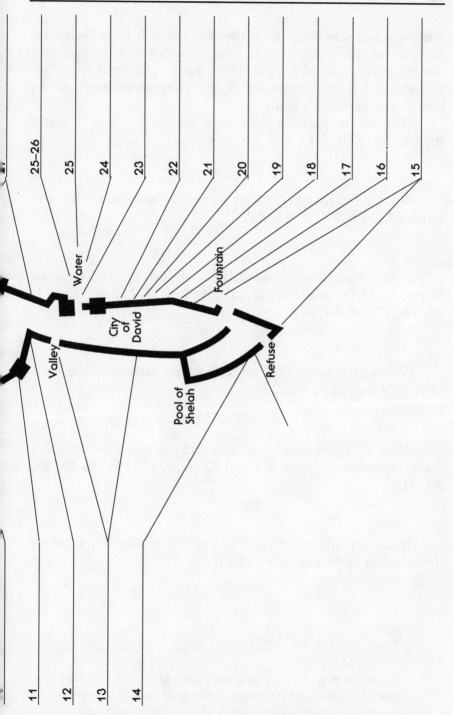

restoring and renewing the walls of the city. It is unlikely that anyone but Nehemiah could have come close to organizing the reconstruction as he did. Only the official registry of the builders and their parts in the bigger picture can begin to do justice to Nehemiah's plan.

Who set the pace for the rest of the builders and how did they do it? (Neh. 3:1)

What different professions were represented among the builders? (Neh. 3:1, 8, 17, 22, 31, 32)

What other towns and villages of Judah and Benjamin helped build the walls of Jerusalem? (Neh. 3:2, 5, 7, 13, 14, 15, 16, 17, 18, 19, 27)

Which groups repaired more than one section of the wall? (Neh. 3:4 and 21, 5 and 27)

What are the names of the gates rebuilt under Nehemiah's construction plan? (Neh. 3:1 and 32, 3, 6, 13, 14, 15, 26, 28, 29, 31)

What are the unusual features about the work crews described in Nehemiah 3:5 and 12?

AT A GLANCE

On the map of Nehemiah's Jerusalem, fill in the blanks with names of workers who repaired that portion of the wall. Numbers by blanks are verses in Nehemiah 3 where names are found.

BEHIND THE SCENES

Nehemiah 3 reveals a remarkable display of unity. Some forty groups worked simultaneously. On the eastern and southeastern sides a whole new wall had to be constructed, and on the northwest and southwest the older wall needed to be repaired. Archaeologists have found remnants of Nehemiah's new wall which are eight feet thick. The successful rebuilding demonstrates Nehemiah's great ability to lead and organize. It also foreshadows unity of purpose and work that is to characterize the church (Phil. 1:27, 28).[2]

KINGDOM EXTRA

We must come to the point at which we acknowledge that the completion of our growth is going to have to involve other brothers and sisters in Christ. In restoring the human personality, I come to terms with the fact that just as Jerusalem's wall would never have been completed without each Jew partnering with the rest, so *I* am only going to be put together through interrelationships with other members of the body of Christ. As Nehemiah led these ancient Jews in a rebuilding partnership, the Holy Spirit wants to lead us in relationships to one another.[3]

FAITH ALIVE

Nehemiah grouped his workers by families, communities, or occupations. What spiritual strength do you draw from fellowship and service with other Christians who are close to you and similar to you?

Priests (Neh. 3:1) worked next to goldsmiths and merchants (v. 31) to complete the walls of Jerusalem. Diversity reigned between the groups of friends and relatives. How has

God built up your life by putting you in close contact with Christians very different from you?

What would be the advantages for your church if every ethnic, economic, and age group in the community was abundantly represented in its membership? What stands in the way of this happening?

DEFLECTING PHONY PROPAGANDA

The local opponents of the Jews who did not want to see Jerusalem fortified and Judah prosperous had limited options available to them. Nehemiah was connected to the emperor himself (Neh. 1:11). He had letters from Artaxerxes authorizing his mission to Jerusalem in no uncertain terms (2:7, 8). The opponents did have recent history on their side. Within the past ten years they had stopped another wall project by force without the emperor's explicit approval (Ezra 4:17–23). Perhaps they could demoralize the builders to the point they would abandon the project.

How had the reaction of Sanballat and Tobiah intensified each time they heard yet more about Nehemiah's efforts to rebuild Jerusalem's walls? (compare Neh. 2:10, 19; 4:1)

What do you think Sanballat wanted to accomplish in the minds of the Jews by means of each of these actions?

• Massing his army (Neh. 4:2)

• Inviting a guest dignitary to address the troops (Neh. 4:3)

- Inciting the troops with sarcastic ridicule of the Jews and their work (Neh. 4:1–3)

Sanballat asked five taunting questions about the wall-building effort of the Jews. The first two questions mocked their ability to build. The second two mocked the speed with which they were building. The last question mocked the materials they were using. What do you understand Sanballat to be implying about these three topics? (Neh. 4:2)

1. The ability of the Jews to build the walls

2. The speed with which they were building

3. The materials they were using

What did Tobiah's little joke add to Sanballat's ridicule of the effort by Nehemiah and the Jews to rebuild the wall? (Neh. 4:3)

Why do you think Nehemiah reacted to the scare tactics of Sanballat and Tobiah with such a stern and uncompromising prayer for their destruction? (Neh. 4:4, 5)

 BIBLE EXTRA

Nehemiah's strong prayer against his enemies (indeed against the enemies of God) finds several parallels in the Old Testament (for example, Pss. 69:22–28; 94:1–3, 23; 109:1–20; 137:7–9; Jer. 17:18; 18:21–23).

How does Jesus expect His followers to react to their enemies? (Matt. 5:43–48)

What was the apostle Paul's commentary on the teaching of Jesus? (Rom. 12:14–21)

Even though Jesus lifts our prayers for our enemies to a higher level than that of Nehemiah's, what does his prayer illustrate about righteous indignation and commitment to the purposes of God? (Neh. 4:4, 5)

 FAITH ALIVE

In the person of Sanballat, we see in Nehemiah 4 the satanic style of opposition you can expect after the Holy Spirit begins His work in you. As the enemy of Nehemiah's work with the Jews, his words personify Satan's attempts at thwarting *us*.[4]

Sanballat ridiculed the Jews as helpless and frail. How does Satan work in your mind and emotions to make you feel weak and worthless?

Sanballat questioned the value of the worship of the Jews in their unprotected temple. How does Satan work in your mind and heart to make you ashamed of the Lord or ashamed of what you bring Him in worship?

Sanballat wanted the Jews to question whether they had bitten off more than they could chew by attempting to build the whole wall all at once. How does Satan work in your mind and heart to make you think the restoration of your life by the Holy Spirit will never get done?

Sanballat mocked the building material the Jews were using in the wall. He said that the old limestone blocks had been calcined by fire (they hadn't) and would crumble like charcoal briquettes. How does Satan work in your mind and heart to make you doubt that there is anything worthwhile in you for the Holy Spirit to work with?

ANTICIPATING REAL ATTACKS

Once before the enemies of the Jews had used force to keep them from building the walls of Jerusalem (Ezra 4:23). Technically, that force had exceeded imperial authorization (v. 21), but they had gotten away with it. Judah was a long way from Shushan. A lot could happen in the distant province and be ignored as long as the security of the central government wasn't threatened.

What was the critical moment in the construction of the walls when Sanballat and Tobiah felt they had to act decisively to stop the project? (Neh. 4:6)

To what did Nehemiah attribute the early rapid progress of the Jewish builders? (Neh 4:6)

What was the next step of the opponents of Nehemiah and the Jews in their escalating war of nerves? (Neh. 4:7, 8)

 ## BEHIND THE SCENES

The Ashdodites have joined the list of enemies of the Jews. Ashdod had been one of the five Philistine cities (Josh. 13:3; 1 Sam. 6:17). By the time of the Persian Empire, its name was given to the coastal province west of Judah. Now the Jews were totally surrounded: Sanballat's Samaria to the north, Tobiah's Ammon to the east, Geshem's Arabs to the south, and Ashdod to the west.

When Nehemiah and the Jews learned of the four-way conspiracy, what were their responses to it? (Neh. 4:9)

The midpoint of any large project is a dangerous time. A great deal is done, but it's obvious how much remains. Everyone is tired, and it's natural to question whether the goal can be reached. What doubts began to run through the ranks of the wallbuilders at the halfway point? (Neh. 4:10)

What rumors were the opponents circulating to dishearten the builders? (Neh. 4:11)

How were the enemies of the Jews able to plant their messages among the Jews working on the walls of Jerusalem? (Neh. 4:12)

It appears that Nehemiah briefly stopped all construction on the wall to squelch the demoralizing rumors that were originating inside (Neh. 4:10) and outside (v. 11) the project. How did Nehemiah go about counteracting the panic that was starting among the workers?

- Physical countermeasure (Neh. 4:13)

- Verbal countermeasures (Neh. 4:14)

WORD WEALTH

Families (Neh. 4:13) translates a Hebrew noun indicating people bound together by shared kinship. It is broader than the idea of a nuclear family that is typically expressed in Hebrew by the word "house." It is narrower than the terms for "nation" or "tribe."[5] In Ezra and Nehemiah the clans or **families** within Judah, Benjamin, and Levi formed the backbone of social organization. They were the logical divisions for a militia because they would care passionately for one another.

BEHIND THE SCENES

Nehemiah's exhortation to "remember the Lord, great and awesome" (Neh. 4:14) was the only exhortation sufficient to produce such single-minded devotion that they would work beyond sunset (see Deut. 24:15) until the stars were out (Neh. 4:21). The city wall the workers toiled on was more than 1.5 miles in length and approximately eight feet thick.[6]

What was the outcome of Nehemiah's response to the threat of sneak attacks by the Samarians, Ammonites, Arabs, and Ashdodites? (Neh. 4:15)

From the time of the rumored sneak attack until the walls and gates were completed, what were Nehemiah's instructions for each of these groups involved in the project?

- His personal servants (Neh. 4:16)

- The materials carriers (Neh. 4:17)

- The builders (Neh. 4:18)

What was Nehemiah's plan for dealing with any attack that might occur during the balance of the construction project? (Neh. 4:19, 20)

It appears that the men in view in Nehemiah 4:21 and 22 were leading citizens, because they had servants.[7] What did Nehemiah expect of these wealthy men as their special contribution to the security of the wall construction? (Neh. 4:21, 22)

How did Nehemiah and his servants set an example for everyone else laboring on the walls and gates of Jerusalem? (Neh. 4:23)

KINGDOM EXTRA

Nehemiah's direction and equipping of the Jerusalemites for resistance and victory displays timeless principles: (a) The enemy is real, not imaginary; (b) the battle is crucial; defeat or victory is at stake; (c) victory is certain when God's people draw on His resources. The Holy Spirit is your ever-present Comforter, here today to show the way to secure the "city" of your own soul and personal circumstances and bring victory against every satanic onslaught.

Spiritual warfare is no game, but neither is it a realm to fear or attempt to avoid. Paul said of the tactics of the Adversary, "We are not ignorant of his devices" (2 Cor. 2:11). There is no escaping its reality, and there is no running from its implications. People who deny warfare or philosophize about it are already victims of the battle.[8]

FAITH ALIVE

The Jews of Nehemiah's day needed the defense from the Lord that Nehemiah was able to provide for them. Today the armor of God is needed to withstand the assaults of the devil and his demonic horde (Eph. 6:10–20).

How can the truth (Eph. 6:14) protect you from the lying attacks of Satan?

What protection does the breastplate of righteousness (Eph. 6:14) give against "the fiery darts of the wicked one" (v. 16)?

Why do you suppose the "gospel of peace" is footwear for the armor of God? (Eph. 6:15)

How do the shield of faith and the helmet of salvation (Eph. 6:16, 17) go together in preparing us for battle as believers being restored by the Holy Spirit?

How does "the sword of the Spirit which is the word of God" (Eph. 6:17) function as the only necessary offensive weapon in the armor?

Why do you think prayer is the activity for which all the armor of God prepares us? In what ways is prayer synonymous with spiritual warfare?

1. Derek Kidner, *Ezra and Nehemiah: An Introduction and Commentary* (Leicester, England: InterVarsity Press, 1979), 85.

2. *Spirit-Filled Life® Bible* (Nashville: Thomas Nelson Publishers, 1991), 678, note on Neh. 3:1–32.

3. Jack W. Hayford, *Rebuilding the Real You* (Ventura, CA: Regal Books, 1986), 172.

4. Ibid., 179.

5. *Theological Wordbook of the Old Testament,* Vol. II (Chicago: Moody Press, 1980), 947.

6. *Spirit-Filled Life® Bible,* 679, 680, note on Neh. 4:14.

7. H. G. M. Williamson, *Ezra, Nehemiah,* Vol. 16 of *Word Biblical Commentary* (Waco, TX: Word Books, Publisher, 1985), 229.

8. Hayford, *Rebuilding the Real You,* 203.

Lesson 8/A Man Who Is a Winner
Nehemiah 5:1—7:3

In the Indiana Jones movies, it was a telling moment when Harrison Ford's character left his academic world and put on his field archaeology clothes. That sweat-stained hat, that bull whip, and that leather jacket all signaled action for the viewer. Indiana Jones's crooked grin or determined glare let you know he was in control.

No matter what, Indiana Jones had the look of a winner. Split his lip, roll boulders at him, shoot poisoned arrows at him, drop him in pits of rats, spiders, or (worst of all) snakes, and he gets tougher. Indiana Jones is a winner.

It's easy to be a winner in fiction. Real life demands a different kind of hero. Nehemiah was such a real-life hero. He too had the look of a winner. No matter what the opponents of the walls of Jerusalem threw at him, Nehemiah responded with uncanny wisdom, decisiveness, and personal strength. You know as you read the accounts that Satan and his servants were behind the attacks on God's work, and that the Spirit of God was moving in Nehemiah's heart and mind. Still you have to marvel at this man who was so clearly a winner.

GETTING TO THE HEART OF DISUNITY

Nehemiah surely expected to face opposition from surrounding power-brokers who did not want to see Jerusalem become independent of their influence. It was logical to resist Satan from without. When the devil's fingerprints showed up on trouble within the people of God, Nehemiah may have been shocked. Then again, maybe he expected the enemy to work from within as well as from without. Experienced spiritual leaders do.

How did Nehemiah become aware of an internal problem festering within the Jewish community in Jerusalem and Judah? (Neh. 5:1)

What was the complaint of each of these groups?

1. The landless peasants (Neh. 5:2)

2. The small landholders (Neh. 5:3)

3. Larger landholders (Neh. 5:4)

4. All three groups of distressed Jews (Neh. 5:5)

 WORD WEALTH

Live (Neh. 5:2) translates a common Hebrew verb meaning "to breathe," "to be alive," "to recover health," and "to flourish." The fundamental idea is "to live and breathe," breathing being the evidence of life in the Hebrew concept. Hence the nouns for "living being," "animal," and "life" all derive from this verb. The Old Testament resists the idea that mere physical existence is enough. True "living and breathing" is the result of doing the right thing (Deut. 4:1; 30:19; Prov. 4:4; 9:6; Amos 5:4). **Live** has a very fundamental quality in our text, however, where the issue is staying alive physically.[1]

What was Nehemiah's response to the complaint of so many oppressed and desperate fellow countrymen? How did he manage his strong emotions so they did not get him into trouble? (Neh. 5:6, 7)

How did Nehemiah use each of these approaches in clarifying the responsibility for the financial and familial distress in Judah and Jerusalem?

- Private confrontation (Neh. 5:7b)

- Public confrontation (Neh. 5:7c–9)

- Personal repentance (Neh. 5:10)

 KINGDOM EXTRA

Since Nehemiah prefigures the Holy Spirit, some would conceivably suppose the prophet to be incapable of plain, assertive, forthright indignation. But this capacity is not inconsistent with the Holy Spirit Himself, for He is not only characterized by the gentleness of a dove, but also as the Spirit of judgment and burning. Remember that the anger and action of the Holy Spirit seek the ultimate good of the people involved. His assertive vengeance is never vindictive, but confrontational and bold to judge against evil. He won't stand for it, nor will He allow us to willfully, ignorantly push forward unto our own confusion or failure. Since He cares enough to restore us, He cares enough to confront us.[2]

How did Nehemiah use each of these approaches in creating a resolution to the financial and familial distress in Judah and Jerusalem?

- Challenge to make restitution for wrongs done (Neh. 5:11)

- A formal commitment ceremony (Neh. 5:12)

- A curse on non-compliers (Neh. 5:13)

WORD WEALTH

Restore (Neh. 5:11) translates a common Hebrew verb that occurs more than a thousand times in the Old Testament. It is translated more than sixty ways, but the idea behind all of the senses is returning to an original condition. In a spiritual sense, this verb usually means "to repent" (Hos. 3:5), although it can mean to return to the fallen state by "turning away" from God (Num. 14:43). Nehemiah 5:11 contains the sense of restoring the inheritances of the various families of Israel by forgiving debts and freeing slaves.[3]

What was the response of the wealthy Jews who had been taking advantage of their countrymen who were in financial straits to Nehemiah's confrontation to remit all the debts? (Neh. 5:12a, 13c)

What do you think these groups each had to praise the Lord for? (Neh. 5:13)

1. The destitute Jewish families

2. The wealthy Jewish creditors

FAITH ALIVE

How do social distinctions and wealth tend to divide Christians in our churches?

What can we do to reduce the barriers created by money and class?

How do you think the Holy Spirit confronts us when we disregard His restoring work in our personalities in order to pursue our selfish interests?

How can the Spirit's chastening—unpleasant as it may seem—lead to praise in our hearts?

SETTING THE PACE OF SELF-SACRIFICE

From the time that he learned how hard life was for the common people in Judah, Nehemiah accepted the responsibility to be a role model of concern for his Jewish brothers and sisters. The few verses that conclude Nehemiah 5 reveal a staggering personal investment in the future of the people whom God had laid on Nehemiah's heart.

For the first time in the Book of Nehemiah, what do we learn was Nehemiah's position in Judah? (Neh. 5:14)

How long was Nehemiah's first term in this office? (Neh. 5:14)

 KINGDOM EXTRA

Back in Nehemiah 2:6 the Persian emperor Artaxerxes had asked how long a leave of absence Nehemiah wanted to deal with the disgrace of his ancestral city. One of the most moving things in this whole book is to discover that he asked for twelve years!

I can imagine a man asking, "May I have a two-month leave of absence?" or "Well, King, sire, could I possibly have a year?"

But twelve years!

Just as Nehemiah recognized the task would not be accomplished rapidly, the living God has sent His Holy Spirit to work completeness in you—even though it takes time.

And just as the king agreed, so it is today: "The LORD will perfect that which concerns me; Your mercy, O LORD, endures forever" (Ps. 138:8).

Whatever time it takes, He is committed to your completion, and that completed work will be a work of holiness unto the Lord—worked in you by the Holy Spirit of God.[4]

How did each of these groups approach the matter of financing the provincial government of Judah by means of added taxes on the citizenry?

- Nehemiah and his family (Neh. 5:14c)

- All of the former governors of Judah (Neh. 5:15)

Why did Nehemiah take the approach that he should fund his government from his private wealth? (Neh. 5:15c, 18b)

 KINGDOM EXTRA

Leaders must insure the welfare of the church. They are servants, providing examples of obedience and diligence to God's people. Only those who live this way should be entrusted with responsibility.

Leaders, reprove those who ignore the welfare of others, pursuing personal gain. Champion the cause of the poor and needy. Do not lord it over others; devote yourself to working diligently.[5]

How did Nehemiah, his brothers, and his servants sacrifice for the welfare of Judah and Jerusalem in each of these ways?

- By the way they worked on restoring and renewing Jerusalem (Neh. 5:16)

- By being a hospitable governor (Neh. 5:17)

- By being a generous governor (Neh. 5:18)

What kind of memorial did Nehemiah want to endure of his governorship over Judah? (Neh. 5:19)

 FAITH ALIVE

When you contemplate the part of your soul or personality that is in greatest disarray, what does it mean to you that the Spirit of God is more committed to restoring and renewing you than Nehemiah was to Jerusalem?

What does Nehemiah's example also say to you about how you should respond to the restoring and renewing work of the Spirit within you?

How can you show the same self-sacrificial spirit Nehemiah exhibited in the leadership roles you fill?

HANDLING PSYCHOLOGICAL WARFARE

In Nehemiah 4, Jerusalem's wall-builders faced opposition from their surrounding enemies. The assault was aimed at the project in order to intimidate the workers as a group. The next wave of external opposition focused on Nehemiah alone. The wall was nearly completed. The enemies hoped to discredit the leader so that the last stages of renovation would be abandoned in disgust.

The first response of Nehemiah's enemies was a bit of intrigue. At what point in the construction did they become sufficiently desperate to resort to trickery? (Neh. 6:1)

Locate Ono on the map of Judah and Samaria in Lesson 1 and circle it. Based on its location, make some suggestions about why Sanballat and Geshem wanted to lure Nehemiah to that area.

How did Nehemiah evade the attempt by Sanballat and Geshem to lure him into what was surely a trap? (Neh. 6:3)

Why do you think Sanballat and Geshem repeated their offer of a peace conference four times? What impression do you get of them from this persistence? (Neh. 6:4)

When intrigue failed to lure Nehemiah into a trap, Sanballat turned to innuendo. He sent a fifth messenger with a very different message. What was the point of sending this new message as an open letter? (Neh. 6:5)

What charges did Sanballat make against Nehemiah in the form of alleged rumors attributed to many nameless sources and one very prominent source? (Neh. 6:6, 7)

What do you think Sanballat would have accomplished in each of these situations?

1. If the Persians believed Nehemiah was rebelling against Artaxerxes

2. If the Jews believed Nehemiah wanted to become their king

3. If Nehemiah went to Ono to defend himself against Sanballat's letter

How did Nehemiah choose to respond to Sanballat's innuendo? What risks did he run by taking that approach? What benefits do you think he gained from doing this? (Neh. 6:8)

What did Nehemiah conclude was the goal of Sanballat's campaign of innuendo? How did he counter that goal spiritually? (Neh. 6:9)

After intrigue and innuendo failed, Tobiah and Sanballat tried to intimidate Nehemiah.[6] How were they able to get a threat to Nehemiah's ears in such a way that it seemed believable? (Neh. 6:10)

What did Nehemiah's enemies want him to do to avoid an imaginary crisis? Why do you think this would have damaged Nehemiah's reputation among the Jews to the point of making him ineffective? (Neh. 6:10, 13)

Why did Nehemiah reject Shemaiah's "prophecy" so emphatically? (Neh. 6:11)

As he reflected on Shemaiah's strange "prophecy," what did Nehemiah conclude about it? (Neh. 6:12, 13) How do you think he reached this insight?

BEHIND THE SCENES

The invitation of Shemaiah, who may have been a priest, to accept sanctuary in the temple was not an alternative for Nehemiah for two reasons: Since he was not a priest, he could not with impunity enter the Holy Place, and God revealed to him this was a plot on his life.[7]

KINGDOM EXTRA

Wisdom knows that no spiritual progress will go unopposed but will incur spiritual opposition, sometimes expressed through human agency. Therefore, act with discernment. The wise will discern the true origin of many verbal attacks as assaults motivated by our spiritual adversary. They will reject negative prophecy from malignant sources.[8]

What does Nehemiah's prayer about the intrigue, innuendo, and intimidation of his enemies reveal about these topics? (Neh. 6:14)

- His confidence in God's justice

- His confidence in his discernment

- His confidence in his calling

FAITH ALIVE

What have you learned from the example of Nehemiah about the value of focusing on your goals as a way of overcoming opposition?

What have you learned from the example of Nehemiah about how to react to rumors and false reports that may be spread about you?

What have you learned from the example of Nehemiah about how to pray about the need for discernment during times of opposition?

THE COLD WAR AFTER THE HOT ONE

Incredibly, the walls of Jerusalem were completed and the gates were hung. As a counterpoint to the joy that must have flowed from that occasion, an undercurrent of nagging opposition to Nehemiah sounded throughout the months and years of Nehemiah's governorship in Judah.

How long did the construction of the walls of Jerusalem take? (Neh. 6:15)

What impact did the speed of the wall construction have on the enemies of God's people? Why was this so? (Neh. 6:16)

    BEHIND THE SCENES

Elul (Neh. 6:15) was the sixth month of the year that began with the month Nisan noted in Nehemiah 2:1. All of the events of chapters two through six crowded into that half a year. Elul occurs in the fall, roughly September–October of a solar calendar. The twenty-fifth day of Elul that year fell on October 2.[9] Construction would have begun on August 12.

Which of Nehemiah's enemies became the greatest threat after the walls were done? How did he exert his influence? (Neh. 6:17)

How had Tobiah inveigled his way into Judean society? (Neh. 6:18)

What role had Meshullam, the son of Berechiah, played in Nehemiah's story besides giving his daughter in marriage to Tobiah's son? (Neh. 6:18; see 3:4)

How did all of Tobiah's contacts and influence put pressure on Nehemiah to compromise the truth of God with this one who probably combined worship of the Lord with worship of pagan gods? (Neh. 6:19)

Nehemiah did not let Tobiah or anything else distract him from what was most important. Before he gave any thought to celebrating the amazing feat of building the walls, he further strengthened the security of Jerusalem. In the absence of a large population in Jerusalem, who did Nehemiah appoint to guard the city gates? (Neh. 7:1)

Who did Nehemiah designate as the security supervisors of the guards, and why did he select them over others? (Neh. 7:2; see 1:2, 3)

What extra security measures did Nehemiah impose to make the gates even more formidable to anyone considering causing trouble? (Neh. 7:3)

FAITH ALIVE

What spiritual resources must a leader depend on when opposition won't go away even after he or she has led God's people into great achievements?

For what sorts of things should you pray with regard to your pastor and other church leaders as they deal with the kind of opposition that spiritual leaders always face?

Who in your church or circle of Christian friends can people count on to be alert to dangers from the world, the flesh, and the devil?

1. *Spirit-Filled Life® Bible* (Nashville: Thomas Nelson Publishers, 1991), 1342, "Word Wealth, Hab. 2:4, shall live."

2. Jack W. Hayford, *Rebuilding the Real You* (Ventura, CA: Regal Books, 1986), 209, 210.

3. *Spirit-Filled Life® Bible*, 393, "Word Wealth, Ruth 4:15, restorer."

4. Hayford, *Rebuilding the Real You*, 90, 91.

5. *Spirit-Filled Life® Bible*, 694, "Truth-in-Action through Nehemiah."

6. Edwin M. Yamauchi, "Ezra-Nehemiah," *The Expositor's Bible Commentary*, Vol. 4 (Grand Rapids: Zondervan Publishing House, 1988), 712.

7. *Spirit-Filled Life® Bible*, 681, note on Neh. 6:1–14.

8. Ibid., 694, "Truth-in-Action through Nehemiah."

9. Ibid., 682, note on Neh. 6:15–19.

Restoring and Renewing Faithfulness
(Nehemiah 7:4—13:31)

Whenever you hear someone mention Nehemiah in a sermon or Sunday school class, it's because he built the walls of Jerusalem. That's not what he wanted to be remembered for. His first concern was the spiritual well-being of his people (Neh. 1:2) and the distress and shame they lived in. The walls were important only because their absence left the Jews vulnerable to their ever-watchful enemies.

Accordingly, there was no celebration in the Book of Nehemiah immediately after the walls were completed. It had to wait until the spiritual restoration and renewal occurred. Only then could the freshly reconsecrated people of Judah and Jerusalem properly dedicate the walls. The joy of the Lord—found in His eternal Word—enabled them to deal with the errors of the past and pledge themselves to walk with Him into a hopeful future.

Whenever our lives feel ineffective or stale, whenever we have experienced the chastening of the Lord, whenever we want to reach a greater level of intimacy with our Lord, one of our priorities must be recommitting our hearts and wills to serve God. The Holy Spirit makes His dwelling and His base of operation in hearts loyal to their Lord.

Lesson 9/ Renewal Through God's Word

Nehemiah 7:4—8:18

Something strange and wonderful happened in England during the first half of the seventeenth century, starting when James I was king. It had happened a century earlier on the continent in northern Germany. Private and public morality improved markedly. Marriages and families flourished. Crime dropped. Attitudes changed about God and humanity.

The Bible—the Word of God—had appeared in everyday language. The King James Bible (A.D. 1611) in English recreated the phenomenon Germany experienced when Luther's translation came out (A.D. 1534). English kings, like German princes and barons, might control the pulpits, but they could not muzzle the Word of God read in the homes of peasants, craftsmen, and merchants.

The Word of God is living and powerful. It is seed, containing germs of truth that can grow for years. It is milk that can nourish tender new life and meat for strong, active souls. It's a hammer and fire to get rid of sin and balm to heal the wounds. It's a sword to defeat the devil and honey for the heart.

It's not surprising that when Nehemiah laid down his trowel, he picked up his Bible. Nor is it strange that he turned over center stage to Ezra, the master Bible teacher. Nehemiah—like the Holy Spirit—turned others loose to use their talents to benefit all of God's people.

IT TELLS US WHO WE ARE

It has been said of classical Judaism that it backs into the future, keeping its eyes fixed on the certainties of the past for guidance. Clearly, Nehemiah felt that before the Jews of his day could take their next step they needed to orient themselves to the momentous time nearly a century earlier when the first exiles had returned to Judah and Jerusalem from Babylon.

Once the walls of Jerusalem were completed and put under organized guards, what problem did Nehemiah want to address next? (Neh. 7:4)

How did Nehemiah arrive at these various courses of action reported throughout the first half of the Book of Nehemiah?

• The certainty that he should rebuild the walls of Jerusalem (Neh. 1:4–11; 2:12)

• The details of how to organize the building campaign (Neh. 2:11–16)

• The various responses to external enemies (Neh. 4:4, 5, 9, 20; 6:9b, 12, 14)

• The internal problem of oppression within the Jewish community (Neh. 5:6, 7)

• The need to populate Jerusalem after its walls were built (Neh. 7:5a)

Nehemiah 7:6–73a reproduces rather exactly the list of original settlers found in Ezra 2. It lists leaders (Neh. 7:7); people by clans (vv. 8–25); people by towns (vv. 26–38); priests, Levites, and various temple servants (vv. 39–60); and those who could not establish their lineage (vv. 61–63). Why do you imagine it mattered to the various people of

Nehemiah's day how they related to their ancestors of a century earlier?

Why do you think Nehemiah wanted to be certain everyone knew where they fit into the historical community of Judah and Benjamin before suggesting anyone might move from his ancestral town to Jerusalem? (Neh. 7:6–73a)

Assuming a twenty-eight-day lunar month, how much time passed between the completion of the wall in the sixth month (Neh. 6:15) and the mass assembly Nehemiah convened (7:73b—8:2)?

BIBLE EXTRA

The first day of the seventh month (Neh. 8:2) was the first day of the Jewish religious year (Rosh Hashana). "The months of the year were numbered from the time of the Exodus, but the beginning of the year was celebrated, according to the agricultural cycle, in the seventh month."[1] Look up the following passages and describe the significance according to the Law of the first day of the seventh month.

• Leviticus 23:23–25

• Numbers 29:1–6

Where did the mass assembly of the Jews take place? (Neh. 8:1; see 3:26 and the map in Lesson 7)

Why do you think the Jews who gathered to register their ancestry and mark a new year in their restored capital pointedly requested Ezra the scribe to read the Law to them? (Neh. 8:1)

Notice the very full description of the Law in Nehemiah 8:1. What does each part of the description add to the total picture?

- The Law of Moses

- Which the Lord had commanded

- The Lord had commanded Israel

Who assembled to hear Ezra read the Law? (Neh. 8:2, 3)

It's interesting that Ezra read the Law to the people in a setting other than the temple courtyard. He took the Word of God into the public square instead. What other features of this encounter with the Law are striking? (Neh. 8:3)

 FAITH ALIVE

How do Christians also look to the past for the keenest insights into the present and the future?

How does the Word of God help you understand your identity as a man, woman, or child?

How does our interest or disinterest in hearing the Word
of God act as a barometer of our spiritual condition?

IT TELLS US WHAT GOD WANTS

Once the people of Judah and Jerusalem had been assured
that they were among the covenant people of God with an
inheritance in the land, the next question was what the Lord
expected of them. Old Testament believers who did not have
personal copies of the Word of God often surprise us with their
unfamiliarity with the details of the Law. They were dependent
on the priests and Levites fulfilling their roles as teachers
(Deut. 33:10).

What details of the Law-reading ceremony reveal that
Ezra must have been anticipating the request by the assembly
of Jews to read the Law of the Lord to them? (Neh. 8:4, 7)

The people on the elevated platform with Ezra are not
identified beyond their names. They may have been priests or
lay leaders of the nation or a combination of the two. Why do
you imagine it was important that more leaders than Ezra alone
stood behind the proclamation of God's Law? (Neh. 8:4)

When Ezra unrolled the scroll on which the Law of God
was written, the assembly responded to it in several ways. What
do you think each of these responses reveal about the attitudes
of the Jews toward the Lord, His Law, and themselves? (Neh.
8:5, 6)

• They stood up

• They raised their hands and called out, "Amen, Amen!"

- They prostrated themselves

What do you think it added to this public reading of the Law for Ezra to bless the Lord before reading on His behalf to the assembly? (Neh. 8:6)

As Ezra read from the Law over a period of approximately six hours, he apparently paused at times during which the thirteen Levites (the expression "and the Levites" in verse 7 probably means "even the Levites"²) moved about doing their job. What was the role of the Levites? (Neh. 8:7, 8)

 WORD WEALTH

Understand (Neh. 8:3, 7, 8, 12, 13) is the key word of Nehemiah 8. It translates a Hebrew verb that occurs roughly 165 times in the Old Testament with reference to the intelligent process of perception, discernment, and understanding that all humans display in varying amounts. The noun **understanding** (v. 2) derives from this verb. In the present reference, spiritual revival could not come until the people listening to Ezra and his levitical assistants fully grasped the meaning and the personal and corporate implications of God's Word.³

What was the response of the assembly of Jews when they heard and understood the Law of God as read by Ezra and explained by the Levites? Why do you suppose they responded that way? (Neh. 8:9)

Why do you suppose Nehemiah stepped back into a leadership role when it was time to guide the people in the appropriate way to respond to the Law? (Neh. 8:9)

Why do you think Nehemiah, Ezra, and the Levites wanted the people to respond to the holy day with joy rather than mourning? (Neh. 8:9)

How did Nehemiah want the people to celebrate that holy day, the first day of the seventh month? (Neh. 8:10; see Num. 29:1–6)

 KINGDOM EXTRA

Living God's way means making God's priorities our priorities, realizing that they are often different from ours. God still accomplishes all things through His Word. Therefore, the Scriptures are a guide for ordering our lives according to God's will. Understanding and obeying them brings joy. Cultivate and promote the joy of the Lord among God's people as a powerful source of spiritual strength.[4]

Joy is the pulse beat to the heart of the message that has resounded since the birth of Christ: "Behold, I bring you good tidings of great joy which will be to all people. For there is born to you this day in the city of David a Savior, who is Christ the Lord" (Luke 2:10, 11).

The news is *good*:	"I bring you *good* tidings
The joy is *great*:	of *great* joy to all people
The focus is *you*:	for to *you*
The time is *now*:	is born *this day* a Savior
And God is *here*:	who is Christ the *Lord!*"[5]

Why do you think the occasion required the assistance of the Levites to change the emotional tone of the event? (Neh. 8:11)

What Nehemiah had urged on the Jews "took account of elementary facts of life: the little luxuries that can turn a meal into a feast, but also the caring and love which can turn simple gaiety into the joy of the Lord."[6] What made the celebration of these Jews distinct from happy ritual? (Neh. 8:12)

 FAITH ALIVE

How important have you found your attitude toward the Word of God to be on the occasions when it has spoken powerfully to you?

What all do you think is included in the idea of understanding God's Word besides an intellectual grasp of its content?

Why is it more fundamental to spiritual reality and worship to celebrate God's grace than to mourn your sins?

IT TELLS US HOW TO WORSHIP GOD

At the heart of spiritual living is worship of God. Worship isn't an hour-a-week activity on Sunday morning. It is responding whenever and wherever appropriate to every recognition of the majesty of God the Father, Son, and Holy Spirit. The Jews came away from Ezra's marathon Bible reading with a hunger for this kind of worship.

How did the leaders of the various clans in Judah and Benjamin follow up on the mass rally of the first day of the seventh month? (Neh. 8:13)

What did the executive-level Bible study focus on in the Law of God? (Neh. 8:14)

BIBLE EXTRA

The Feast of Tabernacles was one of three pilgrimage feasts (Deut. 16:16) that Israelites were expected to observe at the central sanctuary (first the tabernacle and later the temple in Jerusalem). Because the Feast of Trumpets and the Day of Atonement also fell in the seventh month, this season became the favorite time of pilgrimage to Jerusalem.

The Feast of Tabernacles was a dual celebration. Identify its two purposes from the following Scriptures.

1. (Lev. 23:39, 40)

2. (Lev. 23:42, 43)

What kinds of offerings were to be offered for the entire nation during the Feast of Tabernacles? (Num. 29:12–38)

Who was to celebrate the Feast of Tabernacles? (Deut. 16:14)

What occasional feature of the Feast of Tabernacles made it the perfect time for Ezra and Nehemiah's revival based on the reading of the Law? (Deut. 31:10–13)

What role did the leaders who had studied with Ezra about the Feast of Tabernacles play in facilitating its celebration that year? (Neh. 8:15)

How did the Jews from all around Judah and Benjamin carry out their leaders' instructions concerning the Feast of Tabernacles? (Neh. 8:16, 17a; refer to the map in Lesson 7)

There had been regular observances of the Feast of Tabernacles through the years (for example, 1 Kin. 8:2, 65; Ezra 3:4; Zech. 14:16). What do you think may have set this celebration apart from all the previous ones and made it the greatest? (Neh. 8:17b)

What was the unique feature of Ezra and Nehemiah's Feast of Tabernacles? How did this exceed the mandate for every seventh year in Deuteronomy 31:10–13? (Neh. 8:18)

As the Jews of Nehemiah's day reenacted the wilderness wandering of their ancestors who had left Egypt, what do you think it added to their worship and celebration to be reminded of the Law that those ancestors had been the first to hear?

 BEHIND THE SCENES

The Feast of Tabernacles is enjoying a resurgence of popularity among Jews around the world under its Hebrew name *Succoth* or *Sukkoth*. *Sukkoth* is the plural of *sukkah*, the word for "booth" or "hut." You can see little leafy booths on a New York City apartment balcony or witness massive celebrations in Israel.[7]

 FAITH ALIVE

What insights into worshiping the Lord have you gained from this portion of God's Word about the celebration of the Feast of Tabernacles in 445 B.C.?

How does the Word of God speak to you differently in private worship and in public worship?

The worship the Jews engaged in during the Feast of Tabernacles prepared them for an intense experience of confession and soul-searching (Neh. 9). How does worship and the Word of God prepare you to face your sins and deal with them from a repentant heart?

1. *Spirit-Filled Life® Bible* (Nashville: Thomas Nelson Publishers, 1991), 239, note on Num. 29:1–6.

2. Mark Roberts, *Ezra, Nehemiah, Esther,* Vol. 11 of *Mastering the Old Testament* (Dallas: Word Books, Publisher, 1993), 245, note 1.

3. *Spirit-Filled Life® Bible,* 684, "Word Wealth, Neh. 8:8, understand."

4. Ibid., 693, "Truth-in-Action through Nehemiah."

5. Jack W. Hayford, *Rebuilding the Real You* (Ventura, CA: Regal Books, 1986), 228, 229.

6. Derek Kidner, *Ezra and Nehemiah: An Introduction and Commentary* (Leicester, England: InterVarsity Press, 1979), 107.

7. *Spirit-Filled Life® Bible,* 685, note on Neh. 8:13–18.

Lesson 10/Renewal Through Confession and Commitment
Nehemiah 9—10

A little boy came running into the kitchen where his mother was preparing dinner. His sister was right behind him. "Susie hit me!" he blurted out, trying to cry a little for effect.

"He hit me first," Susie shrilled in self-defense.

"Is that right, Billy?" his mother asked.

"Yes, but I had to. She called me a toad face."

"But he called me a booger head."

Mother sent them both to their rooms.

Parents who have gone around and around like this with small children know there is a world of difference between a reluctant admission of guilt and a true confession. Confession tells the truth with conviction and without excuse. In the spiritual realm confession begins with telling the truth about God and only then moves to telling the truth about me. I confess my faith in God before I can confess my sins.

When Nehemiah and Ezra led the Jews of Judah and Jerusalem in confession and recommitment, they followed precisely this pattern. In fact Nehemiah 9 had profound influence on the pattern of confession that developed in the synagogues of Judaism.[1]

ADMITTING THE PAST

Before praying about the present, the assembled Jews surveyed their history with remarkable candor about their "perpetual guilt" and even more remarkable faith in the Lord's "perpetual grace."[2] Their prayer is shot through with allusions and references to the events of the Law of God. They had been listening well to Ezra and the Levites.

The Feast of Tabernacles ran from the fifteenth through the twenty-second days of the seventh month (Lev. 23:34–36). How much time passed between the end of the feast and the gathering of Nehemiah 9:1?

In contrast to the joy of the Feast of Tabernacles (see Neh. 8:10), what emotions and actions marked the new assembly? (Neh. 9:1)

What was the purpose of the assembly on the twenty-fourth day of the seventh month? (Neh. 9:2)

Why was it logically necessary for Israelites to separate from pagans to do this? (Neh. 9:2)

What two activities did the assembly of Jews consider to be essential preliminaries before they could make adequate confession of past and present sins? (Neh. 9:3)

    WORD WEALTH

Confessed (Neh. 9:2, 3) translates a Hebrew verb that means "to throw, cast" in its simplest forms. In its complex forms this verb means to throw out a true estimation of. When applied to God, this verb often means "to praise" and appears in the Psalms parallel to *halal*, the root of *hallelu-Yah*. When used of people, this verb usually refers to throwing out a true estimation of sin, that is, confession. A particularly intensive form of the Hebrew verb appears in contexts of national confession, such as Ezra 9, Nehemiah 9, and Daniel 9.[3]

What did the first group of seven Levites lead the people in doing to introduce the period of public confession? (Neh. 9:4)

Look up Judges 6:6; 1 Samuel 4:13; and Jeremiah 47:2; determine what this verb for "crying out" (Neh. 9:4) usually implied.

What did the second group of seven Levites lead the people in doing to introduce the period of public confession? (Neh. 9:5a)

Who is the subject of every sentence in the first section of the public confession by the assembled Jews? (Neh. 9:5b–16)

What did the Jews confess about the Lord in relation to each of these topics?

- Creation (Neh. 9:6)

- The call of Abram/Abraham (Neh. 9:7, 8)

- The Exodus from Egypt (Neh. 9:9–12)

- Coming down on Mount Sinai (Neh. 9:13–15)

Contrast the ancestors of the Jews and the Lord in the following situations.

THE ISRAELITES   THE LORD

Keeping the covenant
(Neh. 9:16, 17a)   (Neh. 9:17b)

Wilderness wandering
(Neh. 9:18)   (Neh. 9:19–21)

Conquest of the Promised Land
(Neh. 9:25)   (Neh. 9:22–24)

Period of the judges
(Neh. 9:26)   (Neh. 9:27)

Period of the kings and prophets
(Neh. 9:28a, c)   (Neh. 9:28b, d–31)

 FAITH ALIVE

What are some of the worldly practices and attitudes you have to separate yourself from because they tend to pull you away from telling the truth about your sins?

What experiences have demonstrated to you that the Lord is "slow to anger, abundant in kindness"? (Neh. 9:17)

What individual acts or patterns of disobedience in your past serve to remind you of your perpetual need of God's grace?

FACING THE PRESENT

The Jews of Nehemiah's day realized that the distress they were in was a direct result of the disobedience of their ancestors at the time of the Babylonian captivity. Their prayer for the present was rooted firmly in the past. At the same time, their hope for the present and future sprang from what they confessed about God's past faithfulness.

     KINGDOM EXTRA

The power-packed word "confess" opens a great truth concerning God's hearing and answering prayers. To confess belief is to say, "I openly receive God's promise and choose to take my stand here, humbly, on God's promises and in worship of His Person." *Yadah*, the Hebrew word for "confess," contains and supports this idea. Derived from *yad*, meaning "an open or extended hand," the focus is on reaching to take hold of.

Yadah also involves worship, with open, extended hands, in a worship-filled confessing of God's faithfulness with thanksgiving and praise. This is the true spirit of the idea of "faith's confession of God's Word": (1) to take a stand on what God says; (2) to speak what is believed with worship and praise; and (3) to do so in the humble spirit of faith in God's Person and promise. Such a stance will never be loveless or arrogant, and neither earth nor hell can successfully protest this confession of faith in heaven's power.[4]

Nehemiah 9:32 is the main statement of petition in this prayer of the Jews. Summarize these parts of it.

- Address to God

- Request of God

- Those who have suffered

- The time of distress

What fundamental truths did the Jews confess about God and themselves as they looked to the present and future? (Neh. 9:33–35)

 KINGDOM EXTRA

Few principles are more essential to our understanding than this one: the *presence* of God's kingdom power is directly related to the practice of God's *praise*. It was essential that the Jews of Nehemiah's day enthrone the Lord with praise in the midst of their confession. Wherever God's people exalt His name, He is ready to manifest His kingdom's power in the way most appropriate to the situation, as His rule is invited to invade our setting.

It is this fact that properly leads many to conclude that, in a very real way, praise prepares a *specific* and *present* place for God among His people. Some have chosen the term "establish His throne" to describe this. We do not manipulate God, but align ourselves with the great kingdom truth: *His* is the power, ours is the privilege (and responsibility) to welcome Him into our world—our private, present world or the circumstances of our society.[5]

What bitter irony troubled the Jews whose immediate ancestors had returned from Babylon to the land God had given their distant ancestors? (Neh. 9:36, 37)

WORD WEALTH

Pleasure (Neh. 9:37) translates a Hebrew noun that denotes the will of God or of humans carried out to His or their satisfaction.[6] Because of the sins of their ancestors, the Jews of Nehemiah's day found themselves subject to the **pleasure** of Persian emperors and satraps instead of the **pleasure** of God.

What did the Jews propose doing from their side in conjunction with their petition, that God would have regard for the oppression they were experiencing in the land God had given their ancestors? (Neh. 9:38)

FAITH ALIVE

When you approach God in confession, what qualities of His character should you remember and focus on as you pray for His help in living for Him?

Much of the focus of the prayer by the Jews was on the blessings of the Promised Land that their ancestors had forfeited through their disobedience. What spiritual blessings do you think we miss out on when we live in disobedience?

If you were renewing your commitment to the Lord Jesus at this time, what kinds of promises would you make Him in response to His mercy and faithfulness to you?

PROMISING TO REJECT SIN

The sure agreement that the Jews of Nehemiah's day made with the Lord (Neh. 9:38) was not a new covenant. It was a renewal of the covenant the Lord had made with Israel at Mount Sinai as they fled from Egypt in the Exodus. The exilic community in Judah and Jerusalem viewed themselves as the people of a second Exodus. It was fitting that they should vow to restore and renew their devotion to God's covenant.

There is an "and" linking the names in Nehemiah 10:1 and separating them from the people in verse 2. Who were the two men—one familiar and one unknown—who signed the covenant renewal document as the secular rulers of Judah? (Neh. 10:1)

How many priests signed the covenant renewal on behalf of all the priests? (Neh. 10:2–8)

How many Levites signed the covenant renewal document on behalf of all the Levites and temple servants? (Neh. 10:9–13)

How many heads of clans within Judah and Benjamin signed the covenant renewal document on behalf of their kinsmen? (Neh. 10:14–27)

BEHIND THE SCENES

The leaders who attached their names to the covenant renewal document did so by means of seals. They did not sign their names with pen and ink. They pressed signet rings, cylinders, or stamps into wax or other soft substances that would harden on the portion of the scroll set aside for the signatories to the covenant.

How generally does it seem to you that the ordinary citizens of Judah and Jerusalem supported their leaders in renewing the covenant between themselves and the Lord? What gives you this impression? (Neh. 10:28, 29)

Which expressions in Nehemiah 10:28, 29 describe the covenant between the Lord and His people? What recent events had sensitized them to the nature and content of this covenant?

WORD WEALTH

Statute translates the Hebrew noun *choq*, which refers to a defined boundary, especially when written into law, but sometimes not in written form, as in God's limits for the sea and for the rain (Prov. 8:29; Job 28:26). In this passage *choq* appears with *mitzvah* (commandment or precept), *torah* (instruction or law), and *mishpat* (judgment or regulation). *Choq* appears about 220 times in the Old Testament (21 times in Psalm 119 alone). The messianic *choq* (decree), which the Lord Jesus is destined to declare, is world dominion for God's only begotten Son (Ps. 2:7–9).[7]

What would be the role of each of these in obligating the Jews of Nehemiah's days to obey the terms of their covenant with the Lord? (Neh. 10:29)

- A curse

- An oath

In addition to obligating themselves to all the Law of the Lord given by Moses, the Jews of Nehemiah's day singled out certain provisions to stress or clarify in terms of their specific circumstances. What two provisions did they highlight to ensure their separation from pagan influence and corruption?

1. (Neh. 10:30)

2. (Neh. 10:31a)

 KINGDOM EXTRA

The privilege of becoming an authorized and empowered representative of God's kingdom and of ministering Christ's life and the Holy Spirit's gifts to others is not the heritage of the unholy. First Corinthians 6:9, 10 twice says certain people will not "inherit the kingdom of God" and then designates broad categories of people who are excluded from enjoying the resources and rewards of righteousness.

Although our righteousness before God is through Christ's work alone, and while it remains timelessly true that we cannot earn any spiritual gift or right to function in the power of the Holy Spirit, integrity and morality of character are nonetheless essential to the "kingdom person."[8]

How were the Jews declaring their separation from worldliness by promising to obey God's laws about leaving the land fallow and forgiving debts every seven years? (Neh. 10:31b; see Lev. 25:2–4; Deut. 15:1, 2)

FAITH ALIVE

What do you think are the most dangerous influences of the world on God's people today? Why do you think so?

What are some of the limits you need to set for yourself to avoid these sinful influences?

In the space below, write a promise to God about avoiding sin that you know you should keep and sign your name to it. Be thoughtful and careful about what you promise.

PROMISING TO EMPHASIZE WORSHIP

When Nehemiah led the people of Judah and Jerusalem in building the walls of the city in 445 B.C., the temple of the Lord had been standing seventy years. The priests and Levites knew by then how the Jews would or would not support the worship of the Lord. Interestingly, the covenant renewal spelled out a number of provisions to strengthen popular support of the temple and the worship leaders.

The Law did not spell out a way of raising money for a central sanctuary. How did the Jews of Nehemiah's day arrange to meet the monetary needs of the temple? (Neh. 10:32)

How would this money be spent? (Neh. 10:33)

WORD WEALTH

Make atonement (Neh. 10:33) translates the Hebrew verb *chaphar*, which literally means "to cover." When Noah was instructed to "cover" the ark with pitch (Gen. 6:14) this is the word that appears. By extending the idea to include the covering of sins by the blood of sacrificial animals, *chaphar* means "to make atonement, appease God's anger." The noun formed from this verb, *kippur* (atonement), appears in the phrase *Yom Kippur*, Day of Atonement.[9]

The Law did not specify how wood would be gathered for the fires under the temple sacrifices. How did the Jews of Nehemiah's day address this need? (Neh. 10:34)

BEHIND THE SCENES

The firstfruits and the tithes that the people pledged to bring to the temple (Neh. 10:35–39) were not the same thing. Firstfruits represented the earliest of any crop and firstborn animals (Ex. 23:19). They were given to the priests in recognition that everything that followed also came from the Lord as a gracious gift to His people (Num. 18:12–19). Firstborn children were presented to the Lord symbolically and "ransomed" back with money (Ex. 13:12, 13). A second term for firstfruits appears in verse 37. It implies first in quality as well as time. Both kinds of firstfruits were small amounts; tithes on the other hand were substantial contributions of 10 percent of all agricultural produce. Tithes belonged to the Levites, who in turn tithed to the priests (Num. 18:21–28). These grains and other foodstuffs were kept in the storerooms of the temple (Neh. 10:37).

What promises did the Jews of Nehemiah's day make about the firstfruits of their crops, herds, and children? (Neh. 10:35–37a)

What promises did the Jews of Nehemiah's day make about their tithes? (Neh. 10:37b, 38)

What was the goal of all of this elaborate legislation about firstfruits and tithes? (Neh. 10:39)

BEHIND THE SCENES

The prophet Malachi ministered in approximately the same time span as Nehemiah. Read the following passages and summarize the attitudes toward giving to the Lord that the renewed covenant was correcting.

- Malachi 1:7, 8, 12–14

- Malachi 3:8–11

KINGDOM EXTRA

A reliable sign that a person is growing in understanding and commitment is seen in his or her obedience in the area of finances. In the kingdom of God, a spiritual release is connected to our giving patterns.[10]

FAITH ALIVE

The covenant requirements about worship stressed willing participation on the part of everyone in the covenant community. How could you improve your willing, vital participation in the worship activities of your church?

Are there aspects of worship that you tend to dismiss as useless to you? If so, why do you think your church leaders include these worship elements? What may you be missing out on by discounting these aspects of worship?

Are you sowing sparingly or bountifully through your giving to the work of the Lord (2 Cor. 9:6, 7)? How could your giving become a more joyous aspect of your worship of the Lord?

1. Edwin M. Yamauchi, "Ezra-Nehemiah," *The Expositor's Bible Commentary*, Vol. 4 (Grand Rapids: Zondervan Publishing House, 1988), 737.

2. Mark Roberts, *Ezra, Nehemiah, Esther*, Vol. 11 of *Mastering the Old Testament* (Dallas: Word Books, Publisher, 1993), 254.

3. *Theological Wordbook of the Old Testament*, Vol. I, (Chicago: Moody Press, 1980), 365, 366.

4. *Spirit-Filled Life® Bible* (Nashville: Thomas Nelson Publishers, 1991), 619, "Kingdom Dynamics, 2 Chr. 6:24–31, The Meaning of 'Faith's Confession.'"

5. Ibid., 770, 771, "Kingdom Dynamics, Ps. 22:3, 'Establishing' God's Throne."

6. *Theological Wordbook of the Old Testament*, Vol. II, 859, 860.

7. *Spirit-Filled Life® Bible*, 686, "Word Wealth, Neh. 9:13, statutes."

8. Ibid., 1726, "Kingdom Dynamics, 1 Cor. 6:9, 10, Integrity and Morality."

9. Ibid., 217, "Word Wealth, Num. 15:25, make atonement."

10. *Hayford's Bible Handbook* (Nashville: Thomas Nelson Publishers, 1995), 121, note on Neh. 10:37.

Lesson 11/Renewal Through Accepting Challenges
Nehemiah 11:1—13:3

When Winston Churchill was named prime minister of England in place of Neville Chamberlain during the early days of World War II, prospects for victory were dim. Churchill stirred the nation by promising them nothing but blood and tears in the days ahead. He fearlessly strode the bombed-out streets of London with his cigar clamped between his teeth in defiance of danger from the air, and the citizens of the capital and the countryside rallied behind their prime minister.

One of the British who accepted the challenge of hard work to defeat the Germans was a teenager named Elizabeth. The daughter of King George VI donned dungarees and drove a truck to support the war effort. England went on to win the Battle of Britain in the air over their homeland. In time other allies, including the United States, played major roles in the war, but for a time in 1940 the English stood virtually alone and persevered because they accepted the challenge of their bulldog prime minister.

Nehemiah, like Churchill, hated half measures. He wanted to complete what he started. Building walls wasn't enough; the nation needed to renew its covenant with God. A renewed covenant wasn't enough; he wanted to make Jerusalem and Judah model communities where citizens were prosperous and secure while they kept the covenant. Nehemiah issued the challenge, and the Jews responded.

GROWING INTO A BLESSING

The city wall Nehemiah led the Jews in rebuilding enclosed a smaller area than the city the Babylonians had destroyed nearly 140 years earlier. Still the city was underpopulated. The walls were like a pair of jeans bought for an eleven-year-old. They were intentionally too big and needed to be grown into. You can't stop the eleven-year-old, but the Jews would have to grow into Jerusalem on purpose at great effort.

How had Nehemiah described Jerusalem right after the walls were completed? (Neh. 7:4)

What had been Nehemiah's preliminary step toward figuring out how to populate Jerusalem? (Neh. 7:5a)

After the spiritual revival that resulted in covenant renewal, the people were ready to make their communities working expressions of God's Law. One part of that involved accepting the challenge to send residents to Jerusalem. Who already lived in the capital? (Neh. 11:1a)

What means did the Jews use to decide who would move from their ancestral inheritances to Jerusalem so the capital could be a successful city? (Neh. 11:1b)

What was another way Jerusalem received residents? (Neh. 11:2)

BEHIND THE SCENES

The verb "to bless" is usually applied to God in the Old Testament when people give a blessing. Occasionally, people bless other people, but it is unusual (for instance, 1 Chr. 16:2; 2 Chr. 6:3; 30:27). That the Jews blessed their countrymen who volunteered to live in Jerusalem indicates how much sacrifice was involved in leaving ancestral inheritances established at the time of Joshua and the conquest in order to make Jerusalem a strong city.

BIBLE EXTRA

Twice in Nehemiah 11 Jerusalem is referred to as "the holy city" (vv. 1, 18). This designation usually occurs in prophetic passages rather than historical ones. Look up the following verses and summarize what the expression "the holy city" meant to its author.

- Isaiah 48:2; 52:1

- Daniel 9:24

- Joel 3:17

Why do you think chapter 11 is a better place in the Book of Nehemiah for Jerusalem to be called "the holy city" than at the end of chapter 6 when the walls were first completed?

Since Nehemiah could not list everyone who moved into Jerusalem, whose names did he include on his roster? (Neh. 11:3a)

WORD WEALTH

Possession (Neh. 11:3) translates a Hebrew noun that refers to something obtained, seized, or held. Usually in the Old Testament **possession** indicates the land of Israel or, as here, individual portions of it assigned permanently by Joshua to the tribes and families of Israel. (In Psalm 2:8 God promises His Messiah the remotest part of the Earth for His **possession**.[1]) In Nehemiah 11 the minority of Judah and Benjamin (v. 4a) sacrificed the ownership or, at least, the enjoyment of their **possessions** so the majority (v. 3b) could enjoy theirs more fully.

Who were the two leaders of the clan of Perez within the tribe of Judah selected by lot to settle in Jerusalem? (Neh. 11:4b–6)

How many ordinary citizens from Judah were selected or volunteered to help populate Jerusalem? (Neh. 11:6)

Who were the three leaders of the tribe of Benjamin selected by lot to settle in Jerusalem? (Neh. 11:7–8a)

How many ordinary citizens from Benjamin were selected or volunteered to help populate Jerusalem? (Neh. 11:8b)

What surprises you about the comparison between the number of settlers from Judah and Benjamin who moved to Jerusalem to enhance its population? (Neh. 11:6, 8)

Who oversaw the affairs of the new residents of Jerusalem? (Neh. 11:9)

What other leaders did Jerusalem already have? Can you distinguish their functions from those of the new ones in Nehemiah 11:9? (Neh. 3:9, 12; 7:2, 3)

Who were the four leaders among the priests who relocated to Jerusalem? (Neh. 11:10, 11, 14b)

How many ordinary priests were selected or volunteered to help populate Jerusalem from three family groupings? (Neh. 11:12–14a)

Who were the leaders of the Levites for various support ministries for the temple service? (Neh. 11:15, 16)

Who were the leaders of the Levites in matters pertaining to worship? (Neh. 11:17)

How many ordinary Levites were selected or volunteered to repopulate Jerusalem? (Neh. 11:18)

Who led the temple gatekeepers, and how many were there in the new wave of settlers for Jerusalem? (Neh. 11:19)

Who led the Nethinim who moved into Jerusalem, and where in the city did they settle? (Neh. 11:21)

What made Uzzi the Levite and Pethahiah the Judahite so prominent in Jerusalem? (Neh. 11:22–24)

FAITH ALIVE

How do you tend to react to challenges that stretch you and threaten your comfort zone? Do they scare you or excite you?

What is the biggest personal or spiritual challenge facing you right now? How do you need to grow in order to handle it effectively?

What do you think God wants you to learn about Him, about yourself, and about relying on His Spirit from this challenge?

DOING THINGS DECENTLY AND IN ORDER

If you think the lists in Nehemiah have been daunting, wait until you tackle this section of the book. Don't expect to find a name for your next son or grandson (how about Bakbukiah, "The Bottle of the Lord"?). Instead, catch a glimpse of the people of God, freshly inspired by the Word of God, trying to align themselves with God's will expressed through the possessions distributed by Joshua and expressed through the levitical system revealed to Moses and David.

Refer to the map of Judah and Samaria in Lesson 1. How many of the place names pertaining to the tribe of Judah found in Nehemiah 11:25–30 can you locate on that map?

Surprise! All but two of those towns and villages lay farther to the south in Idumean territory that had been part of Judah before the Babylonian captivity. Many families moved outside the official boundaries of Judah to settle on the land God had given their ancestors.

Now, how many of the place names pertaining to the tribe of Benjamin found in Nehemiah 11:31–35 can you locate on the map in Lesson 1?

 BEHIND THE SCENES

North of Jerusalem lay the portion of the Persian province of Judah that was historically the possession of the tribe of Benjamin (Neh. 11:31–35). Many of the place names listed in these verses had impressive histories. Micmash was where Saul and Jonathan fought the Philistines (1 Sam. 14). Aija was the Ai Joshua had difficulty conquering because of Achan's sin (Josh. 7—8). Bethel was where Jacob's ladder reached to the heavens (Gen. 28:10–22). Anathoth was the birthplace of Jeremiah (Jer. 1:1). Ramah was the city of Samuel (1 Sam. 7:17).

There seems to have been a chronic shortage of Levites among those who returned from Babylon. Ezra had to find some for his expedition (Ezra 8:15–20). Censuses always revealed more priests than Levites (Ezra 2:36–42; Neh. 11:10–19). How did the Jews deal with the need for more Levites in Benjamite territory? (Neh. 11:36)

What is the stated significance of the list of priests and list of Levites in Nehemiah 12:1–9 (see Ezra 2:1, 2a)?

Jeshua was high priest when the first Jews returned from Babylon in 538 B.C. Who was high priest in the days of Nehemiah? (Neh. 3:1)

How many generations of high priests are listed in the genealogy of Nehemiah 12:10, 11? How many of them are later than the time of the building of the walls?

The lists of Nehemiah 12 show how carefully the Jews tried to follow the procedures God had established for them in the Law. For them the spirited revival of Nehemiah 8, the soul-stirring confession of Nehemiah 9, the wholehearted recommitment of Nehemiah 10, and the meticulous organization of Nehemiah 12 went together. Spirit did not produce disorder; order did not squelch the Spirit.

The same priestly families who served the Lord when Jeshua was high priest served during the priesthood of Joiakim (Neh. 12:12–21). Did Joiakim serve as high priest before or after the time of Nehemiah? (Neh. 12:10, 11)

Darius II (424–404 B.C.) ruled the Persian Empire after Artaxerxes (464–424 B.C.), the emperor during the lives of Ezra and Nehemiah. How carefully did the Jews keep track of who was authorized to serve as priest and Levite during all these years? (Neh. 12:22, 23)

It's important to note that in most cases these lists record family names rather than the names of the individuals representing the families in a given generation. What glimpses of musical worship and guarding of the temple by some of these ancient families do you find in Nehemiah 12:24 and 25?

The same families that served the Lord when Jeshua was high priest served when Joiakim was priest and when Ezra and Nehemiah did their special works (Neh. 12:26). They would continue to do so for generations to come (vv. 10, 11).

FAITH ALIVE

What routines and disciplines does the Holy Spirit use to give valuable shape and order to your spiritual life?

When does orderliness stop serving the ends of God's Spirit and become a deadening force that impedes spiritual growth?

What can you do to keep order and spontaneity in their proper places in your walk with the Lord?

CLAIMING THE VICTORY

Nehemiah did not record the celebration of the building of Jerusalem's walls until Jerusalem's people were fully restored spiritually and ordered socially. The celebration encompasses much, much more than stones, timbers, and gates. Nehemiah and the Jews joined the psalmist in viewing Jerusalem as the focus of God's rule on earth.

> Walk about Zion,
> And go all around her.
> Count her towers;
> Mark well her bulwarks;
> Consider her palaces;
> That you may tell it to the generation following.
> For this is God,
> Our God forever and ever;
> He will be our guide
> Even to death. (Ps. 48:12–14)

Why did the leaders planning the celebration of the walls of Jerusalem focus on the Levites as crucial to the dedication? (Neh. 12:27, 31, 38, 40–42)

From what you've read in Nehemiah about the distribution of people throughout Judah, why did the leaders have to gather the musicians from so many different places? (Neh. 12:28, 29)

Why do you think the priests purified everyone and everything that would be involved in the dedication ceremony? (Neh. 12:30)

The two choirs seem to have started at the Valley Gate where Nehemiah initiated his nocturnal inspection tour (Neh. 2:13). From there they marched in opposite directions atop the wall of Jerusalem until they met at the northeast corner of the city by the temple (see map of Jerusalem in Lesson 7). Who made up the procession with the first thanksgiving choir, and in what order did they march? (Neh. 12:32–36)

Who made up the procession along with the second thanksgiving choir, and in what order did they march? (Neh. 12:38, 40–42a)

Why was it appropriate for Ezra to lead his procession and for Nehemiah to follow his? (Neh. 12:36b, 38)

BEHIND THE SCENES

In the Hebrew mindset, directions were determined with the assumption that the viewer faced east. Accordingly, "to the right hand" (Neh. 12:31) meant south. "The opposite way" (or to the left) meant north (v. 38). "Before" would mean east and "behind" would mean west.

What were some of the landmarks—familiar from the days of construction—the first choir passed on its route? (Neh. 12:31, 37)

What were some of the landmarks the second choir passed on its route? (Neh. 12:38, 39)

What elements characterized the dedication ceremony of the choirs, priests, leaders, and people in the temple courtyard? (Neh. 12:42b, 43)

KINGDOM EXTRA

Understanding and obeying God's Word brings joy. It also teaches us to acknowledge God's hand in all our successes. Accordingly, we should observe the regular celebration of holy success and spiritual progress. We should dedicate our works to the Lord, knowing it is He who gives all success and progress.[2]

FAITH ALIVE

Nehemiah claimed a victory when he knew God had given him a vision for ministry. He claimed a victory when he courageously challenged God's people to commit themselves to the same vision of ministry. He claimed a victory when he repeatedly refused to yield to enemies who opposed his vision for ministry. He finally claimed a victory when he celebrated the fulfillment of every aspect of his God-given vision for ministry.

What vision do you believe God has planted in your heart for your own life, your family, your church, or some other ministry?

How can you follow the example of Nehemiah in claiming God's victory for this spiritual work?

DARING TO BE THE PEOPLE OF GOD

Nehemiah 12 ends with one example and chapter 13 begins with another of ways the community of Jews in Judah and Jerusalem fulfilled their vow to obey the Law of God and commit themselves to His worship. The ministries of Ezra and Nehemiah were having a lasting impact.

What was the first evidence that the Jews of Judah and Jerusalem were maintaining their loyalty to the Lord and His Law? (Neh. 12:44a)

Why were the Jews so willing to support the priests and Levites generously? (Neh. 12:44b)

In addition to the priests and Levites, what motivated the singers and gatekeepers to do their temple service so willingly? (Neh. 12:45, 46)

Nehemiah compared the willingness of the giving by the Jews in his day to that of their ancestors when they first came from Babylon with extremely high hopes (Neh. 12:47). What was the system of providing for the needs of the servants of the Lord?

BIBLE EXTRA

When the wilderness wanderings were ending and Israel was preparing to invade the land of Canaan, the people massed on the east bank of the Jordan River in Moabite territory. This movement involved battling two Amorite kings and passing through the territories of Edom, Ammon, and Moab (Deut. 2:18, 19, 29). Israel was to treat these related people well by staying on the caravan routes and paying for food and water.

Read Deuteronomy 23:3–6 and summarize the verdict of the Lord on Ammon and Moab based on how they responded to Israel during that time of wandering.

How did the Jews of Nehemiah's day apply the passage in Deuteronomy 23 about Moabites and Ammonites to their situation? (Neh. 13:1–3)

How do you imagine this experience was influenced by Ezra's dealing with marriage to pagan women several years earlier? (see Ezra 9—10)

 KINGDOM EXTRA

The Jews of Nehemiah's day welcomed the kingdom of God into their lives through a balance of receiving His grace and accepting their responsibility. We do the same today. (1) God's sovereignty accomplishes the foundational victory and in the Cross achieves the decisive victory, allowing the saints new dimensions for advance and conquest. (2) He entrusts the responsibility for that advance to His own to "possess the kingdom," entering into conflict with the Adversary, at times at the expense of their apparent defeat. They wrestle the dominion from hellish powers, continuing in warfare until the ultimate seating of the Son of Man.

This age-long struggle between "the saints" and the power of evil in the world calls each believer to a commitment to steadfast battle, a mixture of victories with setbacks, and a consummate triumph anticipated at Christ's coming.[3]

 FAITH ALIVE

What spiritual responsibility that you face do you find most difficult to fulfill?

What motivation do you find in the Word of God and in the joy of your Christian life to dare to pursue this responsibility even though it is difficult for you?

How would the cause of Satan be harmed and the kingdom of God advanced if you dared to be God's man or woman and fulfill that responsibility?

1. *Spirit-Filled Life® Bible* (Nashville: Thomas Nelson Publishers, 1991), 336, "Word Wealth, Josh. 22:9, possession."

2. Ibid., 693, "Truth-in-Action through Nehemiah."

3. Ibid., 1245, "Kingdom Dynamics, Dan. 7:21, 22, Old Testament: Possessing the Kingdom."

Lesson 12/When Renewal Grows Stale
Nehemiah 13:4–31

The 1970s produced a kind of dramatic motion picture that hasn't appealed consistently to later audiences. You don't see a lot of them on Sunday afternoon; occasionally you will in the wee hours when viewers are scarce. Dramatic movies of the 70s were downers. Filmmakers shunned happy endings in favor of "realistic" climaxes in which everything that could went wrong.

Remember *Butch Cassidy and the Sundance Kid*? For ninety minutes the movie invites its viewers to like these two best-buddy misfits who rob trains and banks (without hurting anyone) because they can't find steady work. As the end nears you begin to think they may break free of their past. But this is a 70s movie. In the final scene Butch and Sundance charge into a Bolivian town square to battle a few sleepy militiamen. Unbeknownst to them, most of the Bolivian army is waiting for them. The visual image freezes while volley after volley of rifle fire rings out on the sound track. Butch and Sundance have died hideously even though they are lovable, kindly rascals.

Seventies movies lost the happy ending; and they leave viewers hanging, wanting something more satisfying. The Book of Nehemiah ends that way too (so did the Book of Ezra). Built into these chronologically last words of the Old Testament is a hint that something better was needed by God's people than the Old Covenant. You sense that Nehemiah longed for the power the Holy Spirit brought on Pentecost to believers in Jesus Christ.

WORSHIP NEEDS REVIVING

The final verses of Nehemiah 13 report events that occurred after Nehemiah had completed his twelve-year term as governor of Judah, had gone back to Persia for a time, and then returned to Judah for a second term. All of the special promises made by the Jews during the covenant renewal recounted in chapters 10—12 had been broken. With a mixture of zeal and weariness, Nehemiah tackled the issues once again. As before, he began with worship.

Who was this Eliashib who allied himself with Tobiah, the enemy of the Jews' spiritual health and power? (Neh. 13:4, 28; see 3:1; 12:10, 28)

What spiritual functions had to be sacrificed so that Tobiah the Ammonite official could have personal chambers in the courts of the temple of the Lord? (Neh. 13:5, 10)

How did this action violate the "sure covenant" (Neh. 9:38) the leaders, Levites, priests, and people had made with the Lord shortly after the walls had been constructed? (Neh. 10:35–39)

Where was Nehemiah when Eliashib the priest compromised with the unbelieving bigwigs around him and surrendered the peoples' integrity of and commitment to worship? (Neh. 13:6; see 1:1)

In general terms, how much time had passed since Nehemiah led the Jews in rebuilding the walls of Jerusalem and renewing their commitment to the Lord? (Neh. 13:6; see 2:1; 5:14)

When Nehemiah returned a second time to Jerusalem from Shushan in Persia, he is not identified as entering a second term as governor of Judah. From the way he behaved in Nehemiah 13:4–31, do you think he was or was not the governor again? Why or why not?

BIBLE EXTRA

Compare the action of Nehemiah relative to Tobiah's temple apartment with that of Jesus when He cleansed the temple.

	NEHEMIAH (Neh. 13:8, 9)	JESUS (Matt. 21:12–16)
Motivation		
Method		
Goal		

WORD WEALTH

Cleanse translates a Hebrew verb meaning "to make clean," "to purify," "to be pure, clean, or uncontaminated." This verb and its related adjective are used for cleansing physically, ceremonially, and morally. They can, therefore, refer to pure gold (Ex. 25:11), pure offerings (Lev. 14:4), and a pure heart (Ps. 51:10).[1] Nehemiah ordered the ceremonial cleansing of not only the one room Tobiah had commandeered but of surrounding rooms as well.

What had the Levites done when the temple storerooms no longer supplied their daily material needs? What impact do you imagine this had on the spiritual life of the Jews? (Neh. 13:10)

Why do you suppose Nehemiah held the heads of families responsible for the deterioration of support for the temple rather than the priests and Levites? (Neh. 13:11a)

What part would each of these steps play in stabilizing the temple service?

1. Physically gathering the Levites from the countryside and getting them back at their posts (Neh. 13:11b)

2. Restarting the flow of tithes and firstfruits into the temple storerooms (Neh. 13:12)

3. Appointing a dependable watchdog committee over the collection and distribution of tithes and firstfruits (Neh. 13:13)

If Hanan was a layman, what kind of membership did Nehemiah appoint to the commission to distribute tithes? What do you think he hoped to achieve with this variety? (Neh. 13:13)

  KINGDOM EXTRA

We must be generous toward God's work first, making the care of His servants a high priority. Avoid any tendency to neglect the work of God in favor of personal concerns or selfish ambitions.[2]

Why do you think Nehemiah was concerned that his good deeds toward the temple and the worship of God were in danger of being wiped out? (Neh. 13:14)

When Nehemiah asked God to "remember" him (Neh. 13:14), was he afraid the Lord would forget him or does divine remembrance have a more action-oriented component? How do you reach this conclusion?

FAITH ALIVE

What do you think made the difference between Nehemiah's spiritually successful association with a powerful unbeliever (Artaxerxes) and Eliashib's spiritually disastrous association with a powerful unbeliever (Tobiah)? What can you learn from this about your own relationships with unbelievers?

What tends to happen to your pattern of private and public worship when your devotion to the Lord grows stale?

When your loyalty to the Lord grows stale, do you tend to miss worship and long to be closer to the Lord or do you tend to resist the advances of the Holy Spirit? What does it take to break through your spiritual staleness?

DISTINCTIVES NEED REEMPHASIS

When the Jews had renewed a "sure covenant" (Neh. 9:38) with the Lord, they had clarified certain issues of Sabbath observance as distinctives that would mark them as God's covenant people (10:31). What had been a minor problem at that time—a mere trickle of Sabbath commerce—was a flood when Nehemiah returned from Persia.

What kinds of things had the Jews begun doing on the Sabbath in violation of the Law of God? (Neh. 13:15; see Ex. 20:10)

What kinds of things were resident Phoenicians from Tyre doing on the Sabbath in violation of the "sure covenant" the Jews had renewed several years earlier? (Neh. 13:16; see 10:31a)

How did Nehemiah respond to each of these situations?

• The Sabbath commerce of the Jews (Neh. 13:15b)

• The Sabbath commerce of the local Phoenicians (Neh. 13:17, 18)

 BIBLE EXTRA

Thirty years had passed since Ezra's initial ministry concerning the Sabbath, and people had begun to violate the day in the gap before Nehemiah's second term as governor.[3] Nehemiah identified Sabbath-breaking for profit as one of the sins of Israel that had led to the Babylonian captivity and all the grief the Jews of his day were trying to overcome (see Neh. 9:36, 37). Look up the following passages from the prophets that Nehemiah may have had in mind, and summarize what they had told earlier generations about the Sabbath.

Jeremiah 17:19–27

Ezekiel 20:12–24

What measures did Nehemiah take to ensure that the Jews stuck to the terms of the curse and oath (Neh. 10:29) they had entered relative to the Sabbath? (Neh. 13:19)

What measures did Nehemiah take to ensure that the Gentile merchants accustomed to Sabbath business in Jerusalem didn't torpedo his efforts to jump-start renewed enthusiasm for the Sabbath? (Neh. 13:21, 22a)

Nehemiah's second prayer for remembrance by the Lord includes a plea that he would be spared (Neh. 13:22b). Do you think he was being overly pessimistic or just realistic about the future of the Jews? Why do you conclude this?

 FAITH ALIVE

How do you express in the pattern of your life that serving the Lord is more important than making money? How could you strengthen this aspect of your witness to the world?

The word translated "mercy" with reference to God (Neh. 13:2b) is the same word translated in the plural "good deeds" with reference to Nehemiah (v. 14). It's a covenant term that denotes the loyal love of the parties who obligate themselves to one another. If you were going to pray today about the greatest burden you are bearing in terms of the loyal love between you and the Lord, what would you say in that prayer?

HOLINESS NEEDS TO REASSERT ITSELF

The little enclave of Jews living in Jerusalem and the surrounding countryside faced absorption by its neighbors. Certainly physical absorption was a possibility if the Jews intermarried freely with surrounding people, but spiritual absorption was the more serious danger. Ezra had warned of this (Ezra 9—10). Nehemiah had included this issue in the covenant renewal (Neh. 10:30).

Why was Nehemiah so concerned about intermarriage between the men of Judah and women of Ashdod, Ammon, and Moab? (Neh. 13:23; see v. 1 and 4:7)

What specific evidence of intermarriage with pagan women troubled Nehemiah most deeply? (Neh. 13:24; see Mal. 2:15)

From the context of Ezra-Nehemiah and the example of Solomon's downfall Nehemiah cited, why do you think he reacted so violently against those who had taken pagan wives? (Neh. 13:25)

WORD WEALTH

Cursed translates a Hebrew verb whose root meaning is "to be light or slight." In its intensive forms this verb has the idea of making someone insignificant by lowering their status or position. In technical passages it means to **curse** someone, thereby making them insignificant. Nehemiah acted on his **curse** by publicly demeaning the guilty parties with blows and hair pulling. This word differs sharply from the term used in Nehemiah 10:29 which is a stern, covenantal word of destruction.[4]

What made Solomon's involvement with pagan wives so tragic, and how did his example apply to the Jews of Nehemiah's day? (Neh. 13:26, 27)

KINGDOM EXTRA

True holiness is active and dynamic, not passive and static. We must actively remove the ways of the world from our lives. This involves willingness to root out worldly ways and reject carnal compromises that can diminish the lives of our churches as well as our personal lives. We must refuse evil alliances and, above all, not marry unbelievers.[5]

Who was the most serious offender in the matter of marrying pagan wives? (Neh. 13:28)

How did Nehemiah deal with the adult grandson of the high priest who had married a pagan wife? (Neh. 13:28, 29)

In what sense did Nehemiah want the Lord to "remember" the family of Eliashib the high priest? (Neh. 13:29)

BIBLE EXTRA

The prophet Malachi, who ministered at roughly the same time as Nehemiah, also addressed problems within the priesthood. Read Malachi 2:4–8 and answer the following questions.

How did Levi respond in days of old when the Lord covenanted with him and his descendants that they should be priests? (Mal. 2:4–6)

How should a priest approach his service as a mediator between the Lord and His people? (Mal. 2:7)

How were the priests of Malachi and Nehemiah's day failing in their attitudes and actions? (Mal. 2:8)

What actions did Nehemiah take to get the priesthood and levitical orders functioning in a manner free from any pagan contamination? (Neh. 13:30, 31a; see 10:28, 34)

How does Nehemiah's final prayer for remembrance differ from the two earlier ones in this chapter? Does he seem more hopeful or less hopeful about the success of his reforms? How do you reach that conclusion? (Neh. 13:31b; see vv. 14, 22b)

FAITH ALIVE

At what points are you most vulnerable to influence by the world? How can this influence dull your zeal for the Lord?

How does the Lord remind you when you need to separate yourself from worldly influences that will harm your spiritual health?

How do you think prolonged worldliness results in a curse of insignificance on believers who ignore the conviction of the Holy Spirit?

AN EZRA-NEHEMIAH CHECKLIST

The brief biblical books of Ezra and Nehemiah cap the recorded history of the Old Testament era. Nehemiah's "reforming zeal, partnered by the educative thoroughness of Ezra, gave to postexilic Israel a virility and clarity of faith which it never wholly lost."[6] There are vital lessons for us as followers of Jesus Christ if we too are to have strong, focused faiths and lives.

Read the following key verses from Ezra and Nehemiah. After reading each, meditate on it briefly and write down a personal response to the spiritual truth it presents to you.

- Ezra 1:2–5

- Ezra 2:68, 69

- Ezra 3:2, 3, 10, 11

- Ezra 4:1–3

- Ezra 5:1, 2

- Ezra 6:14, 21, 22

- Ezra 7:10

- Ezra 8:22, 23

- Ezra 9:5, 6

- Ezra 10:1–3

- Nehemiah 1:11

- Nehemiah 2:17, 18

- Nehemiah 4:13, 14

- Nehemiah 6:15, 16

- Nehemiah 8:5–8

- Nehemiah 8:10

- Nehemiah 9:16, 17

- Nehemiah 10:28, 29

- Nehemiah 11:1, 2

- Nehemiah 12:27, 43

- Nehemiah 13:14, 22b, 31b

 FAITH ALIVE

In what way(s) would you like to be more like Ezra?

In what way(s) would you like to be more like Nehemiah?

1. *Spirit-Filled Life® Bible* (Nashville: Thomas Nelson Publishers, 1991), 165, "Word Wealth, Lev. 14:31, cleansed."
2. Ibid., 694, "Truth-in-Action through Nehemiah."
3. Ibid., 692, note on Neh. 13:15–22.
4. *Theological Wordbook of the Old Testament,* Vol. II (Chicago: Moody Press, 1980), 800.
5. *Spirit-Filled Life® Bible,* 693, "Truth-in-Action through Nehemiah."
6. Derek Kidner, *Ezra and Nehemiah: An Introduction and Commentary* (Leicester, England: InterVarsity Press, 1979), 133.

SPIRIT-FILLED LIFE® BIBLE DISCOVERY GUIDE SERIES

*Coming Soon

SPIRIT-FILLED LIFE® KINGDOM DYNAMICS STUDY GUIDES

OTHER SPIRIT-FILLED LIFE® STUDY RESOURCES